# The Free Press

&

# The Historic Thames

**Hilaire Belloc**

**The Free Press & The Historic Thames**

ISBN: 978-1-64799-995-7

# CONTENTS

# DEDICATION

Kings Land,
Shipley, Horsham.
October 14, 1917.

My Dear Orage,

I dedicate this little essay to you not only because "The New Age" (which is your paper) published it in its original form, but much more because you were, I think, the pioneer, in its modern form at any rate, of the Free Press in this country. I well remember the days when one used to write to "The New Age" simply because one knew it to be the only paper in which the truth with regard to our corrupt politics, or indeed with regard to any powerful evil, could be told. That is now some years ago; but even to-day there is only one other paper in London of which this is true, and that is the "New Witness." Your paper and that at present edited by Mr. Gilbert Chesterton are the fullest examples of the Free Press we have.

It is significant, I think, that these two papers differ entirely in the philosophies which underlie their conduct and in the social ends at which they aim. In other words, they differ entirely in religion which is the ultimate spring of all political action. There is perhaps no single problem of any importance in private or in public morals which the one would not attempt to solve in a fashion different from, and usually antagonistic to, the other. Yet we discover these two papers with their limited circulation, their lack of advertisement subsidy, their restriction to a comparatively small circle, possessing a power which is not only increasing but has long been quite out of proportion to their numerical status.

Things happen because of words printed in "The New Age" and the "New Witness." That is less and less true of what I have called the official press. The phenomenon is worth analysing. Its intellectual interest alone will arrest the attention of any future historian. Here is a force numerically quite small, lacking the one great obvious power of our time (which is the power to bribe), rigidly boycotted—so much so that it is hardly known outside the circle of its immediate adherents and quite unknown abroad. Yet this force is doing work—is creating—at a moment when almost everything else is marking time; and the work it is doing grows more and more apparent.

The reason is, of course, the principle which was a commonplace with antiquity, though it was almost forgotten in the last modern generation, that truth has a power of its own. Mere

1

indignation against organized falsehood, mere revolt against it, is creative.

It is the thesis of this little essay, as you will see, that the Free Press will succeed in its main object which is the making of the truth known.

There was a moment, I confess, when I would not have written so hopefully.

Some years ago, especially after I had founded the "Eye-Witness," I was, in the tedium of the effort, half convinced that success could not be obtained. It is a mood which accompanies exile. To produce that mood is the very object of the boycott to which the Free Press is subjected.

But I have lived, in the last five years, to see that this mood was false. It is now clear that steady work in the exposure of what is evil, whatever forces are brought to bear against that exposure, bears fruit. That is the reason I have written the few pages printed here: To convince men that even to-day one can do something in the way of political reform, and that even to-day there is room for something of free speech.

I say at the close of these pages that I do not believe the new spirit we have produced will lead to any system of self-government, economic or political. I think the decay has gone too far for that. In this I may be wrong; it is but an opinion with regard to the future. On the other matter I have experience and immediate example before me, and I am certain that the battle for free political discussion is now won. Mere knowledge of our public evils, economic and political, will henceforward spread; and though we must suffer the external consequences of so prolonged a regime of lying, the lies are now known to be lies. True expression, though it should bear no immediate and practical fruit, is at least now guaranteed a measure of freedom, and the coming evils which the State must still endure will at least not be endured in silence. Therefore it was worth while fighting.

Very sincerely yours,
H. Belloc

# THE FREE PRESS

I propose to discuss in what follows the evil of the great modern Capitalist Press, its function in vitiating and misinforming opinion and in putting power into ignoble hands; its correction by the formation of small independent organs, and the probably increasing effect of these last.

## I

About two hundred years ago a number of things began to appear in Europe which were the fruit of the Renaissance and of the Reformation combined: Two warring twins.

These things appeared first of all in England, because England was the only province of Europe wherein the old Latin tradition ran side by side with the novel effects of protestantism. But for England the great schism and heresy of the sixteenth century, already dissolving to-day, would long ago have died. It would have been confined for some few generations to those outer Northern parts of the Continent which had never really digested but had only received in some mechanical fashion the strong meat of Rome. It would have ceased with, or shortly after, the Thirty Years War.

It was the defection of the English Crown, the immense booty rapidly obtained by a few adventurers, like the Cecils and Russells, and a still smaller number of old families, like the Howards, which put England, with all its profound traditions and with all its organic inheritance of the great European thing, upon the side of the Northern Germanies. It was inevitable, therefore, that in England the fruits should first appear, for here only was there deep soil.

That fruit upon which our modern observation has been most fixed was Capitalism.

Capitalism proceeded from England and from the English Reformation; but it was not fully alive until the early eighteenth century. In the nineteenth it matured.

Another cognate fruit was what to-day we call Finance, that is, the domination of the State by private Capitalists who, taking advantage of the necessities of the State, fix an increasing mortgage upon the State and work perpetually for fluidity, anonymity, and irresponsibility in their arrangements. It was in England, again, that this began and vigorously began with what I think was the first true

3

"National Debt"; a product contemporary in its origins with industrial Capitalism.

Another was that curious and certainly ephemeral vagary of the human mind which has appeared before now in human history, which is called "Sophistry," and which consists in making up "systems" to explain the world; in contrast with Philosophy which aims at the answering of questions, the solution of problems and the final establishment of the truth.

But most interesting of all just now, though but a minor fruit, is the thing called "The Press." It also began to arise contemporaneously with Capitalism and Finance: it has grown with them and served them. It came to the height of its power at the same modern moment as did they.

Let us consider what exactly it means: then we shall the better understand what its development has been.

## II

"The Press" means (for the purpose of such an examination) the dissemination by frequently and regularly printed sheets (commonly daily sheets) of (1) news and (2) suggested ideas.

These two things are quite distinct in character and should be regarded separately, though they merge in this: that false ideas are suggested by false news and especially by news which is false through suppression.

First, of News:—

News, that is, information with regard to those things which affect us but which are not within our own immediate view, is necessary to the life of the State.

The obvious, the extremely cheap, the universal means of propagating it, is by word of mouth.

A man has seen a thing; many men have seen a thing. They testify to that thing, and others who have heard them repeat their testimony. The Press thrust into the midst of this natural system (which is still that upon which all reasonable men act, whenever they can, in matters most nearly concerning them) two novel features, both of them exceedingly corrupting. In the first place, it gave to the printed words a rapidity of extension with which repeated spoken words could not compete. In the second place, it gave them a mechanical similarity which was the very opposite to the marks of healthy human news.

I would particularly insist upon this last point. It is little understood and it is vital.

4

If we want to know what to think of a fire which has taken place many miles away, but which affects property of our own, we listen to the accounts of dozens of men. We rapidly and instinctively differentiate between these accounts according to the characters of the witnesses. Equally instinctively, we counter-test these accounts by the inherent probabilities of the situation.

An honest and sober man tells us that the roof of the house fell in. An imaginative fool, who is also a swindler, assures us that he later saw the roof standing. We remember that the roof was of iron girders covered with wood, and draw this conclusion: That the framework still stands, but that the healing fell through in a mass of blazing rubbish. Our common sense and our knowledge of the situation incline us rather to the bad than to the good witness, and we are right. But the Press cannot of its nature give a great number of separate testimonies. These would take too long to collect, and would be too expensive to collect. Still less is it able to deliver the weight of each. It, therefore, presents us, even at its best when the testimony is not tainted, no more than one crude affirmation. This one relation is, as I have said, further propagated unanimously and with extreme rapidity. Instead of an organic impression formed at leisure in the comparison of many human sources, the reader obtains a mechanical one. At the same moment myriads of other men receive this same impression. Their adherence to it corroborates his own. Even therefore when the disseminator of the news, that is, the owner of the newspaper, has no special motive for lying, the message is conveyed in a vitiated and inhuman form. Where he has a motive for lying (as he usually has) his lie can outdo any merely spoken or written truth.

If this be true of news and of its vitiation through the Press, it is still truer of opinions and suggested ideas.

Opinions, above all, we judge by the personalities of those who deliver them: by voice, tone, expression, and known character. The Press eliminates three-quarters of all by which opinion may be judged. And yet it presents the opinion with the more force. The idea is presented in a sort of impersonal manner that impresses with peculiar power because it bears a sort of detachment, as though it came from some authority too secure and superior to be questioned. It is suddenly communicated to thousands. It goes unchallenged, unless by some accident another controller of such machines will contradict it and can get his contradiction read by the same men as have read the first statement.

These general characters were present in the Press even in its infancy, when each news-sheet still covered but a comparatively small circle; when distribution was difficult, and when the audience

5

addressed was also select and in some measure able to criticize whatever was presented to it. But though present they had no great force; for the adventure of a newspaper was limited. The older method of obtaining news was still remembered and used. The regular readers of anything, paper or book, were few, and those few cared much more for the quality of what they read than for its amount. Moreover, they had some means of judging its truth and value.

In this early phase, moreover, the Press was necessarily highly diverse. One man could print and sell profitably a thousand copies of his version of a piece of news, of his opinions, or those of his clique. There were hundreds of other men who, if they took the pains, had the means to set out a rival account and a rival opinion. We shall see how, as Capitalism grew, these safeguards decayed and the bad characters described were increased to their present enormity.

## III

Side by side with the development of Capitalism went a change in the Press from its primitive condition to a worse. The development of Capitalism meant that a smaller and a yet smaller number of men commanded the means of production and of distribution whereby could be printed and set before a large circle a news-sheet fuller than the old model. When distribution first changed with the advent of the railways the difference from the old condition was accentuated, and there arose perhaps one hundred, perhaps two hundred "organs," as they were called, which, in this country and the Lowlands of Scotland, told men what their proprietors chose to tell them, both as to news and as to opinion. The population was still fairly well spread; there were a number of local capitals; distribution was not yet so organized as to permit a paper printed as near as Birmingham, even, to feel the competition of a paper printed in London only 100 miles away. Papers printed as far from London, as York, Liverpool or Exeter were the more independent.

Further the mass of men, though there was more intelligent reading (and writing, for that matter) than there is to-day, had not acquired the habit of daily reading.

It may be doubted whether even to-day the mass of men (in the sense of the actual majority of adult citizens) have done so. But what I mean is that in the time of which I speak (the earlier part, and a portion of the middle, of the nineteenth century), there was

6

no reading of papers as a regular habit by those who work with their hands. The papers were still in the main written for those who had leisure; those who for the most part had some travel, and those who had a smattering, at least, of the Humanities.

The matter appearing in the newspapers was often written by men of less facilities. But the people who wrote them, wrote them under the knowledge that their audience was of the sort I describe. To this day in the healthy remnant of our old State, in the country villages, much of this tradition survives. The country folk in my own neighbourhood can read as well as I can; but they prefer to talk among themselves when they are at leisure, or, at the most, to seize in a few moments the main items of news about the war; they prefer this, I say, as a habit of mind, to the poring over square yards of printed matter which (especially in the Sunday papers) are now food for their fellows in the town. That is because in the country a man has true neighbours, whereas the towns are a dust of isolated beings, mentally (and often physically) starved.

## IV

Meanwhile, there had appeared in connection with this new institution, "The Press," a certain factor of the utmost importance: Capitalist also in origin, and, therefore, inevitably exhibiting all the poisonous vices of Capitalism as its effect flourished from more to more. This factor was subsidy through advertisement.

At first the advertisement was not a subsidy. A man desiring to let a thing be known could let it be known much more widely and immediately through a newspaper than in any other fashion. He paid the newspaper to publish the thing that he wanted known, as that he had a house to let, or wine to sell.

But it was clear that this was bound to lead to the paradoxical state of affairs from which we began to suffer in the later nineteenth century. A paper had for its revenue not only what people paid in order to obtain it, but also what people paid in order to get their wares or needs known through it. It, therefore, could be profitably produced at a cost greater than its selling price. Advertisement revenue made it possible for a man to print a paper at a cost of 2d. and sell it at 1d.

In the simple and earlier form of advertisement the extent and nature of the circulation was the only thing considered by the advertiser, and the man who printed the newspaper got more and more profit as he extended that circulation by giving more reading matter for a better-looking paper and still selling it further and further below cost price.

When it was discovered how powerful the effect of suggestion upon the readers of advertisements could be, especially over such an audience as our modern great towns provide (a chaos, I repeat, of isolated minds with a lessening personal experience and with a lessening community of tradition), the value of advertising space rapidly rose. It became a more and more tempting venture to "start a newspaper," but at the same time, the development of capitalism made that venture more and more hazardous. It was more and more of a risky venture to start a new great paper even of a local sort, for the expense got greater and greater, and the loss, if you failed, more and more rapid and serious. Advertisement became more and more the basis of profit, and the giving in one way and another of more and more for the 1d. or the 1/2d. became the chief concern of the now wealthy and wholly capitalistic newspaper proprietor.

Long before the last third of the nineteenth century a newspaper, if it was of large circulation, was everywhere a venture or a property dependent wholly upon its advertisers. It had ceased to consider its public save as a bait for the advertiser. It lived (in this phase) entirely on its advertisement columns.

## V

Let us halt at this phase in the development of the thing to consider certain other changes which were on the point of appearance, and why they were on the point of appearance.

In the first place, if advertisement had come to be the stand-by of a newspaper, the Capitalist owning the sheet would necessarily consider his revenue from advertisement before anything else. He was indeed compelled to do so unless he had enormous revenues from other sources, and ran his paper as a luxury costing a vast fortune a year. For in this industry the rule is either very great profits or very great and rapid losses—losses at the rate of £100,000 at least in a year where a great daily paper is concerned.

He was compelled then to respect his advertisers as his paymasters. To that extent, therefore, his power of giving true news and of printing sound opinion was limited, even though his own inclinations should lean towards such news and such opinion.

An individual newspaper owner might, for instance, have the greatest possible dislike for the trade in patent medicines. He might object to the swindling of the poor which is the soul of that trade.

8

He might himself have suffered acute physical pain through the imprudent absorption of one of those quack drugs. But he certainly could not print an article against them, nor even an article describing how they were made, without losing a great part of his income, directly; and, perhaps, indirectly, the whole of it, from the annoyance caused to other advertisers, who would note his independence and fear friction in their own case. He would prefer to retain his income, persuade his readers to buy poison, and remain free (personally) from touching the stuff he recommended for pay.

As with patent medicines so with any other matter whatsoever that was advertised. However bad, shoddy, harmful, or even treasonable the matter might be, the proprietor was always at the choice of publishing matter which did not affect him, and saving his fortune, or refusing it and jeopardizing his fortune. He chose the former course.

In the second place, there was an even more serious development. Advertisement having become the stand-by of the newspaper the large advertiser (as Capitalism developed and the controls became fewer and more in touch one with the other) could not but regard his "giving" of an advertisement as something of a favour.

There is always this psychological, or, if you will, artistic element in exchange.

In pure Economics exchange is exactly balanced by the respective advantages of the exchangers; just as in pure dynamics you have the parallelogram of forces. In the immense complexity of the real world material, friction, and a million other things affect the ideal parallelogram of forces; and in economics other conscious passions besides those of mere avarice affect exchange: there are a million half-conscious and sub-conscious motives at work as well.

The large advertiser still mainly paid for advertisement according to circulation, but he also began to be influenced by less direct intentions. He would not advertise in papers which he thought might by their publication of opinion ultimately hurt Capitalism as a whole; still less in those whose opinions might affect his own private fortune adversely. Stupid (like all people given up to gain), he was muddle-headed about the distinction between a large circulation and a circulation small, but appealing to the rich. He would refuse advertisements of luxuries to a paper read by half the wealthier class if he had heard in the National Liberal Club, or some such place, that the paper was "in bad taste."

Not only was there this negative power in the hands of the advertiser, that of refusing the favour or patronage of his advertisements, there was also a positive one, though that only grew up later.

The advertiser came to see that he could actually dictate policy and opinion; and that he had also another most powerful and novel weapon in his hand, which was the suppression of news.

We must not exaggerate this element. For one thing the power represented by the great Capitalist Press was a power equal with that of the great advertisers. For another, there was no clear-cut distinction between the Capitalism that owned newspapers and the Capitalism that advertised. The same man who owned "The Daily Times" was a shareholder in Jones's Soap or Smith's Pills. The man who gambled and lost on "The Howl" was at the same time gambling and winning on a bucket-shop advertised in "The Howl." There was no antagonism of class interest one against the other, and what was more they were of the same kind and breed. The fellow that got rich quick in a newspaper speculation—or ended in jail over it—was exactly the same kind of man as he who bought a peerage out of a "combine" in music halls or cut his throat when his bluff in Indian silver was called. The type is the common modern type. Parliament is full of it, and it runs newspapers only as one of its activities—all of which need the suggestion of advertisement.

The newspaper owner and the advertiser, then, were intermixed. But on the balance the advertising interest being wider spread was the stronger, and what you got was a sort of imposition, often quite conscious and direct, of advertising power over the Press; and this was, as I have said, not only negative (that was long obvious) but, at last, positive.

Sometimes there is an open battle between the advertiser and the proprietor, especially when, as is the case with framers of artificial monopolies, both combatants are of a low, cunning, and unintelligent type. Minor friction due to the same cause is constantly taking place. Sometimes the victory falls to the newspaper proprietor, more often to the advertiser—never to the public.

So far, we see the growth of the Press marked by these characteristics. (1) It falls into the hands of a very few rich men, and nearly always of men of base origin and capacities. (2) It is, in their hands, a mere commercial enterprise. (3) It is economically supported by advertisers who can in part control it, but these are of the same Capitalist kind, in motive and manner, with the owners of the papers. Their power does not, therefore, clash in the main with that of the owners, but the fact that advertisement makes a paper, has created a standard of printing and paper such that no one—save at a disastrous loss—can issue regularly to large numbers news and opinion which the large Capitalist advertisers disapprove.

There would seem to be for any independent Press no possible economic basis, because the public has been taught to expect for 1d. what it costs 3d. to make—the difference being paid by the advertisement subsidy.

But there is now a graver corruption at work even than this always negative and sometimes positive power of the advertiser.

It is the advent of the great newspaper owner as the true governing power in the political machinery of the State, superior to the officials in the State, nominating ministers and dismissing them, imposing policies, and, in general, usurping sovereignty—all this secretly and without responsibility.

It is the chief political event of our time and is the peculiar mark of this country to-day. Its full development has come on us suddenly and taken us by surprise in the midst of a terrible war. It was undreamt of but a few years ago. It is already to-day the capital fact of our whole political system. A Prime Minister is made or deposed by the owner of a group of newspapers, not by popular vote or by any other form of open authority.

No policy is attempted until it is ascertained that the newspaper owner is in favour of it. Few are proffered without first consulting his wishes. Many are directly ordered by him. We are, if we talk in terms of real things (as men do in their private councils at Westminster) mainly governed to-day, not even by the professional politicians, nor even by those who pay them money, but by whatever owner of a newspaper trust is, for the moment, the most unscrupulous and the most ambitious.

How did such a catastrophe come about? That is what we must inquire into before going further to examine its operation and the possible remedy.

# VI

During all this development of the Press there has been present, first, as a doctrine plausible and arguable; next, as a tradition no longer in touch with reality; lastly, as an hypocrisy still pleading truth, a certain definition of the functions of the Press; a doctrine which we must thoroughly grasp before proceeding to the nature of the Press in these our present times.

This doctrine was that the Press was an organ of opinion—that is, an expression of the public thought and will.

Why was this doctrine originally what I have called it, "plausible and arguable"? At first sight it would seem to be neither the one nor the other.

A man controlling a newspaper can print any folly or falsehood he likes. He is the dictator: not his public. They only receive.

Yes: but he is limited by his public.

If I am rich enough to set up a big rotary printing press and print in a million copies of a daily paper the news that the Pope has become a Methodist, or the opinion that tin-tacks make a very good breakfast food, my newspaper containing such news and such an opinion would obviously not touch the general thought and will at all. No one, outside the small catholic minority, wants to hear about the Pope; and no one, Catholic or Muslim, will believe that he has become a Methodist. No one alive will consent to eat tin-tacks. A paper printing stuff like that is free to do so, the proprietor could certainly get his employees, or most of them, to write as he told them. But his paper would stop selling.

It is perfectly clear that the Press in itself simply represents the news which its owners desire to print and the opinions which they desire to propagate; and this argument against the Press has always been used by those who are opposed to its influence at any moment.

But there is no smoke without fire, and the element of truth in the legend that the Press "represents" opinion lies in this, that there is a limit of outrageous contradiction to known truths beyond which it cannot go without heavy financial loss through failure of circulation, which is synonymous with failure of power. When people talked of the newspaper owners as "representing public opinion" there was a shadow of reality in such talk, absurd as it seems to us to-day. Though the doctrine that newspapers are "organs of public opinion" was (like most nineteenth century so-called "Liberal" doctrines) falsely stated and hypocritical, it had that element of truth about it—at least, in the earlier phase of newspaper development. There is even a certain savour of truth hanging about it to this day.

Newspapers are only offered for sale; the purchase of them is not (as yet) compulsorily enforced. A newspaper can, therefore, never succeed unless it prints news in which people are interested and on the nature of which they can be taken in. A newspaper can manufacture interest, but there are certain broad currents in human affairs which neither a newspaper proprietor nor any other human being can control. If England is at war no newspaper can boycott war news and live. If London were devastated by an earthquake no

12

advertising power in the Insurance Companies nor any private interest of newspaper owners in real estate could prevent the thing "getting into the newspapers."

Indeed, until quite lately—say, until about the '80's or so— most news printed was really news about things which people wanted to understand. However garbled or truncated or falsified, it at least dealt with interesting matters which the newspaper proprietors had not started as a hare of their own, and which the public, as a whole, was determined to hear something about. Even to-day, apart from the war, there is a large element of this.

There was (and is) a further check upon the artificiality of the news side of the Press; which is that Reality always comes into its own at last.

You cannot, beyond a certain limit of time, burke reality.

In a word, the Press must always largely deal with what are called "living issues." It can boycott very successfully, and does so, with complete power. But it cannot artificially create unlimitedly the objects of "news."

There is, then, this much truth in the old figment of the Press being "an organ of opinion," that it must in some degree (and that a large degree) present real matter for observation and debate. It can and does select. It can and does garble. But it has to do this always within certain limitations.

These limitations have, I think, already been reached; but that is a matter which I argue more fully later on.

## VII

As to opinion, you have the same limitations.

If opinion can be once launched in spite of, or during the indifference of, the Press (and it is a big "if"); if there is no machinery for actually suppressing the mere statement of a doctrine clearly important to its readers—then the Press is bound sooner or later to deal with such doctrine: just as it is bound to deal with really vital news.

Here, again, we are dealing with something very different indeed from that title "An organ of opinion" to which the large newspaper has in the past pretended. But I am arguing for the truth that the Press—in the sense of the great Capitalist newspapers— cannot be wholly divorced from opinion.

We have had three great examples of this in our own time in England. Two proceeded from the small wealthy class, and one from the mass of the people.

13

The two proceeding from the small wealthy classes were the Fabian movement and the movement for Women's Suffrage. The one proceeding from the populace was the sudden, brief (and rapidly suppressed) insurrection of the working classes against their masters in the matter of Chinese Labour in South Africa.

The Fabian movement, which was a drawing-room movement, compelled the discussion in the Press of Socialism, for and against. Although every effort was made to boycott the Socialist contention in the Press, the Fabians were at last strong enough to compel its discussion, and they have by now canalized the whole thing into the direction of their "Servile State." I myself am no more than middle-aged, but I can remember the time when popular newspapers such as "The Star" openly printed arguments in favour of Collectivism, and though to-day those arguments are never heard in the Press—largely because the Fabian Society has itself abandoned Collectivism in favour of forced labour—yet we may be certain that a Capitalist paper would not have discussed them at all, still less have supported them, unless it had been compelled. The newspapers simply could not ignore Socialism at a time when Socialism still commanded a really strong body of opinion among the wealthy.

It was the same with the Suffrage for Women, which cry a clique of wealthy ladies got up in London. I have never myself quite understood why these wealthy ladies wanted such an absurdity as the modern franchise, or why they so blindly hated the Christian institution of the Family. I suppose it was some perversion. But, anyhow, they displayed great sincerity, enthusiasm, and devotion, suffering many things for their cause, and acting in the only way which is at all practical in our plutocracy—to wit, by making their fellow-rich exceedingly uncomfortable. You may say that no one newspaper took up the cause, but, at least, it was not boycotted. It was actively discussed.

The little flash in the pan of Chinese Labour was, I think, even more remarkable. The Press not only had word from the twin Party Machines (with which it was then allied for the purposes of power) to boycott the Chinese Labour agitation rigidly, but it was manifestly to the interest of all the Capitalist Newspaper Proprietors to boycott it, and boycott it they did—as long as they could. But it was too much for them. They were swept off their feet. There were great meetings in the North-country which almost approached the dignity of popular action, and the Press at last not only took up the question for discussion, but apparently permitted itself a certain timid support.

My point is, then, that the idea of the Press as "an organ of

14

public opinion," that is, "an expression of the general thought and will," is not only hypocritical, though it is mainly so. There is still something in the claim. A generation ago there was more, and a couple of generations ago there was more still.

Even to-day, if a large paper went right against the national will in the matter of the present war it would be ruined, and papers which supported in 1914 the Cabinet intrigue to abandon our Allies at the beginning of the war have long since been compelled to eat their words.

For the strength of a newspaper owner lies in his power to deceive the public and to withhold or to publish at will hidden things: his power in this terrifies the professional politicians who hold nominal authority: in a word, the newspaper owner controls the professional politician because he can and does blackmail the professional politician, especially upon his private life. But if he does not command a large public this power to blackmail does not exist; and he can only command a large public—that is, a large circulation—by interesting that public and even by flattering it that it has its opinions reflected—not created—for it.

The power of the Press is not a direct and open power. It depends upon a trick of deception; and no trick of deception works if the trickster passes a certain degree of cynicism.

We must, therefore, guard ourselves against the conception that the great modern Capitalist Press is merely a channel for the propagation of such news as may suit its proprietors, or of such opinions as they hold or desire to see held. Such a judgment would be fanatical, and therefore worthless.

Our interest is in the degree to which news can be suppressed or garbled, particular discussion of interest to the common-weal suppressed, spontaneous opinion boycotted, and artificial opinion produced.

# VIII

I say that our interest lies in the question of degree. It always does. The philosopher said: "All things are a matter of degree; and who shall establish degree?" But I think we are agreed—and by "we" I mean all educated men with some knowledge of the world around us—that the degree to which the suppression of truth, the propagation of falsehood, the artificial creation of opinion, and the boycott of inconvenient doctrine have reached in the great Capitalist Press for some time past in England, is at least dangerously high.

There is no one in public life but could give dozens of examples from his own experience of perfectly sensible letters to the Press, citing irrefutable testimony upon matters of the first importance, being refused publicity. Within the guild of the journalists, there is not a man who could not give you a hundred examples of deliberate suppression and deliberate falsehood by his employers both as regards news important to the nation and as regards great bodies of opinion.

Equally significant with the mere vast numerical accumulation of such instances is their quality.

Let me give a few examples. No straightforward, common-sense, real description of any professional politician—his manners, capacities, way of speaking, intelligence—ever appears to-day in any of the great papers. We never have anything within a thousand miles of what men who meet them say.

We are, indeed, long past the time when the professional politicians were treated as revered beings of whom an inept ritual description had to be given. But the substitute has only been a putting of them into the limelight in another and more grotesque fashion, far less dignified, and quite equally false.

We cannot even say that the professional politicians are still made to "fill the stage." That metaphor is false, because upon a stage the audience knows that it is all play-acting, and actually sees the figures.

Let any man of reasonable competence soberly and simply describe the scene in the House of Commons when some one of the ordinary professional politicians is speaking.

It would not be an exciting description. The truth here would not be a violent or dangerous truth. Let him but write soberly and with truth. Let him write it as private letters are daily written in dozens about such folk, or as private conversation runs among those who know them, and who have no reason to exaggerate their importance, but see them as they are. Such a description would never be printed! The few owners of the Press will not turn off the limelight and make a brief, accurate statement about these mediocrities, because their power to govern depends upon keeping in the limelight the men whom they control.

Once let the public know what sort of mediocrities the politicians are and they lose power. Once let them lose power and their hidden masters lose power.

Take a larger instance: the middle and upper classes are never allowed by any chance to hear in time the dispute which leads to a strike or a lock-out.

Here is an example of news which is of the utmost possible

importance to the commonwealth, and to each of us individually. To understand why a vast domestic dispute has arisen is the very first necessity for a sound civic judgment. But we never get it. The event always comes upon us with violence and is always completely misunderstood—because the Press has boycotted the men's claims.

I talked to dozens of people in my own station of life—that is, of the professional middle classes—about the great building lock-out which coincided with the outbreak of the War. I did not find a single one who knew that it was a lock-out at all! The few who did at least know the difference between a strike and a lock-out, all thought it was a strike!

Let no one say that the disgusting falsehoods spread by the Press in this respect were of no effect The men themselves gave in, and their perfectly just demands were defeated, mainly because middle-class opinion and a great deal of proletarian opinion as well had been led to believe that the builders' cessation of labour was a strike due to their own initiative against existing conditions, and thought the operation of such an initiative immoral in time of war. They did not know the plain truth that the provocation was the masters', and that the men were turned out of employment, that is deprived of access to the Capitalist stores of food and all other necessaries, wantonly and avariciously by the masters. The Press would not print that enormous truth.

I will give another general example.

The whole of England was concerned during the second year of the War with the first rise in the price of food. There was no man so rich but he had noticed it in his household books, and for nine families out of ten it was the one pre-occupation of the moment. I do not say the great newspapers did not deal with it, but how did they deal with it? With a mass advocacy in favour of this professional politician or that; with a mass of unco-ordinated advices; and, above all, with a mass of nonsense about the immense earnings of the proletariat. The whole thing was really and deliberately side-tracked for months until, by the mere force of things, it compelled attention. Each of us is a witness to this. We have all seen it. Every single reader of these lines knows that my indictment is true. Not a journalist of the hundreds who were writing the falsehood or the rubbish at the dictation of his employer but had felt the strain upon the little weekly cheque which was his own wage. Yet this enormous national thing was at first not dealt with at all in the Press, and, when dealt with, was falsified out of recognition.

I could give any number of other, and, perhaps, minor instances as the times go (but still enormous instances as older

17

morals went) of the same thing. They have shown the incapacity and falsehood of the great capitalist newspapers during these few months of white-hot crisis in the fate of England.

This is not a querulous complaint against evils that are human and necessary, and therefore always present. I detest such waste of energy, and I agree with all my heart in the statement recently made by the Editor of "The New Age" that in moments such as these, when any waste is inexcusable, sterile complaint is the worst of waste. But my complaint here is not sterile. It is fruitful. This Capitalist Press has come at last to warp all judgment. The tiny oligarchy which controls it is irresponsible and feels itself immune. It has come to believe that it can suppress any truth and suggest any falsehood. It governs, and governs abominably: and it is governing thus in the midst of a war for life.

# IX

I say that the few newspaper controllers govern; and govern abominably. I am right. But they only do so, as do all new powers, by at once alliance with, and treason against, the old: witness Harmsworth and the politicians. The new governing Press is an oligarchy which still works "in with" the just-less-new parliamentary oligarchy.

This connection has developed in the great Capitalist papers a certain character which can be best described by the term "Official."

Under certain forms of arbitrary government in Continental Europe ministers once made use of picked and rare newspapers to express their views, and these newspapers came to be called "The Official Press." It was a crude method, and has been long abandoned even by the simpler despotic forms of government. Nothing of that kind exists now, of course, in the deeper corruption of modern Europe—least of all in England.

What has grown up here is a Press organization of support and favour to the system of professional politics which colours the whole of our great Capitalist papers to-day in England. This gives them so distinct a character, of parliamentary falsehood, and that falsehood is so clearly dictated by their connection with executive power that they merit the title "Official."

The regime under which we are now living is that of a Plutocracy which has gradually replaced the old Aristocratic tradition of England. This Plutocracy—a few wealthy interests—in part controls, in part is expressed by, is in part identical with the professional politicians, and it has in the existing Capitalist Press an ally similar to that "Official Press" which continental nations knew in the past. But there is this great difference, that the "Official Press" of Continental experiments never consisted in more than a few chosen organs the character of which was well known, and the attitude of which contrasted sharply with the rest. But our "official Press" (for it is no less) covers the whole field. It has in the region of the great newspapers no competitor; indeed, it has no competitors at all, save that small Free Press, of which I shall speak in a moment, and which is its sole antagonist.

If any one doubts that this adjective "official" can properly be applied to our Capitalist Press to-day, let him ask himself first what the forces are which govern the nation, and next, whether those forces—that Government or regime—could be better served even under a system of permanent censorship than it is in the great dailies of London and the principal provincial capitals.

Is not everything which the regime desires to be suppressed, suppressed? Is not everything which it desires suggested, suggested? And is there any public question which would weaken the regime, and the discussion of which is ever allowed to appear in the great Capitalist journals?

There has not been such a case for at least twenty years. The current simulacrum of criticism apparently attacking some portion of the regime, never deals with matters vital to its prestige. On the contrary, it deliberately side-tracks any vital discussion that sincere conviction may have forced upon the public, and spoils the scent with false issues.

One paper, not a little while ago, was clamouring against the excess of lawyers in Government. Its remedy was an opposition to be headed by a lawyer.

Another was very serious upon secret trading with the enemy. It suppressed for months all reference to the astounding instance of that misdemeanour by the connections of a very prominent professional politician early in the war, and refused to comment on the single reference made to this crime in the House of Commons!

Another clamours for the elimination of enemy financial power in the affairs of this country, and yet says not a word upon the auditing of the secret Party Funds!

I say that the big daily papers have now not only those other qualities dangerous to the State which I have described, but that they have become essentially "official," that is, insincere and corrupt in their interested support of that plutocratic complex which, in the decay of aristocracy, governs England. They are as official in this sense as were ever the Court organs of ephemeral Continental

19

experiments. All the vices, all the unreality, and all the peril that goes with the existence of an official Press is stamped upon the great dailies of our time. They are not independent where Power is concerned. They do not really criticize. They serve a clique whom they should expose, and denounce and betray the generality—that is the State—for whose sake the salaried public servants should be perpetually watched with suspicion and sharply kept in control.

The result is that the mass of Englishmen have ceased to obtain, or even to expect, information upon the way they are governed.

They are beginning to feel a certain uneasiness. They know that their old power of observation over public servants has slipped from them. They suspect that the known gross corruption of Public life, and particularly of the House of Commons, is entrenched behind a conspiracy of silence on the part of those very few who have the power to inform them. But, as yet, they have not passed the stage of such suspicion. They have not advanced nearly as far as the discovery of the great newspaper owners and their system. They are still, for the most part, duped.

This transitional state of affairs (for I hope to show that it is only transitional) is a very great evil. It warps and depletes public information. It prevents the just criticism of public servants. Above all, it gives immense and irresponsible power to a handful of wealthy men—and especially to the one most wealthy and unscrupulous among them—whose wealth is an accident of speculation, whose origins are repulsive, and whose characters have, as a rule, the weakness and baseness developed by this sort of adventures. There are, among such gutter-snipes, thousands whose luck ends in the native gutter, half a dozen whose luck lands them into millions, one or two at most who, on the top of such a career go crazy with the ambition of the parvenu and propose to direct the State. Even when gambling adventurers of this sort are known and responsible (as they are in professional politics) their power is a grave danger. Possessing as the newspaper owners do every power of concealment and, at the same time, no shred of responsibility to any organ of the State, they are a deadly peril. The chief of these men are more powerful to-day than any Minister. Nay, they do, as I have said (and it is now notorious), make and unmake Ministers, and they may yet in our worst hour decide the national fate.

Now to every human evil of a political sort that has appeared in history (to every evil, that is, affecting the State, and proceeding from the will of man—not from ungovernable natural forces outside man) there comes a term and a reaction.

Here I touch the core of my matter. Side by side with what I have called "the Official Press" in our top-heavy plutocracy there has arisen a certain force for which I have a difficulty in finding a name, but which I will call for lack of a better name "the Free Press."

I might call it the "independent" Press were it not that such a word would connote as yet a little too much power, though I do believe its power to be rising, and though I am confident that it will in the near future change our affairs.

I am not acquainted with any other modern language than French and English, but I read this Free Press French and English, Colonial and American regularly and it seems to me the chief intellectual phenomenon of our time.

In France and in England, and for all I know elsewhere, there has arisen in protest against the complete corruption and falsehood of the great Capitalist papers a crop of new organs which are in the strictest sense of the word "organs of Opinion." I need not detain English readers with the effect of this upon the Continent. It is already sufficiently noteworthy in England alone, and we shall do well to note it carefully.

"The New Age" was, I think, the pioneer in the matter. It still maintains a pre-eminent position. I myself founded the "Eye-Witness" in the same chapter of ideas (by which I do not mean at all with similar objects of propaganda). Ireland has produced more than one organ of the sort, Scotland one or two. Their number will increase.

With this I pass from the just denunciation of evil to the exposition of what is good.

I propose to examine the nature of that movement which I call "The Free Press," to analyse the disabilities under which it suffers, and to conclude with my conviction that it is, in spite of its disabilities, not only a growing force, but a salutary one, and, in a certain measure, a conquering one. It is to this argument that I shall now ask my readers to direct themselves.

# X

The rise of what I have called "The Free Press" was due to a reaction against what I have called "The Official Press." But this reaction was not single in motive.

Three distinct moral motives lay behind it and converged upon it. We shall do well to separate and recognize each, because each has had it's effect upon the Free Press as a whole, and that Free Press bears the marks of all three most strongly to-day.

The first motive apparent, coming much earlier than either of the other two, was the motive of (A) Propaganda. The second motive was (B) Indignation against the concealment of Truth, and the third motive was (C) Indignation against irresponsible power: the sense of oppression which an immoral irresponsibility in power breeds among those who are unhappily subject to it.

Let us take each of these in their order.

# XI

## A

The motive of Propaganda (which began to work much the earliest of the three) concerned Religions, and also certain racial enthusiasms or political doctrines which, by their sincerity and readiness for sacrifice, had half the force of Religions.

Men found that the great papers (in their final phase) refused to talk about anything really important in Religion. They dared do nothing but repeat very discreetly the vaguest ethical platitudes. They hardly dared do even that. They took for granted a sort of invertebrate common opinion. They consented to be slightly coloured by the dominating religion of the country in which each paper happened to be printed—and there was an end of it.

Great bodies of men who cared intensely for a definite creed found that expression for it was lacking, even if this creed (as in France) were that of a very large majority in the State. The "organs of opinion" professed a genteel ignorance of that idea which was most widespread, most intense, and most formative. Nor could it be otherwise with a Capitalist enterprise whose directing motive was not conversion or even expression, but mere gain. There was nothing to distinguish a large daily paper owned by a Jew from one owned by an Agnostic or a Catholic. Necessity of expression compelled the creation of a Free Press in connection with this one motive of religion.

Men came across very little of this in England, because England was for long virtually homogeneous in religion, and that religion was not enthusiastic during the years in which the Free Press arose. But such a Free Press in defence of religion (the pioneer of all the Free Press) arose in Ireland and in France and elsewhere. It had at first no quarrel with the big official Capitalist Press. It took for granted the anodyne and meaningless remarks on Religion which appeared in the sawdust in the Official Press, but it asserted

22

the necessity of specially emphasizing its particular point of view in its own columns: for religion affects all life.

This same motive of Propaganda later launched other papers in defence of enthusiasms other than strictly religious enthusiasms, and the most important of these was the enthusiasm for Collectivism—Socialism.

A generation ago and more, great numbers of men were persuaded that a solution for the whole complex of social injustice was to be found in what they called "nationalizing the means of production, distribution, and exchange." That is, of course, in plain English, putting land, houses, and machinery, and stores of food and clothing into the hands of the politicians for control in use and for distribution in consumption.

This creed was held with passionate conviction by men of the highest ability in every country of Europe; and a Socialist Press began to arise, which was everywhere free, and soon in active opposition to the Official Press. Again (of a religious temper in their segregation, conviction and enthusiasm) there began to appear (when the oppressor was mild), the small papers defending the rights of oppressed nationalities.

Religion, then, and cognate enthusiasms were the first breeders of the Free Press.

It is exceedingly important to recognize this, because it has stamped the whole movement with a particular character to which I shall later refer when I come to its disabilities.

The motive of Propaganda, I repeat, was not at first conscious of anything iniquitous in the great Press or Official Press side by side with which it existed. Veuillot, in founding his splendidly fighting newspaper, which had so prodigious an effect in France, felt no particular animosity against the "Debats," for instance; his particular Catholic enthusiasm recognized itself as exceptional, and was content to accept the humble or, at any rate, inferior position, which admitted eccentricity connotes. "Later," these founders of the Free Press seemed to say, "we may convert the mass to our views, but, for the moment, we are admittedly a clique: an exceptional body with the penalties attaching to such." They said this although the whole life of France is at least as Catholic as the life of Great Britain is Plutocratic, or the life of Switzerland Democratic. And they said it because they arose after the Capitalist press (neutral in religion as in every vital thing) had captured the whole field.

The first Propagandists, then, did not stand up to the Official Press as equals. They crept in as inferiors, or rather as open excentrics. For Victorian England and Third Empire France falsely proclaimed the "representative" quality of the Official Press.

To the honour of the Socialist movement the Socialist Free Press was the first to stand up as an equal against the giants.

I remember how in my boyhood I was shocked and a little dazed to see references in Socialist sheets such as "Justice" to papers like the "Daily Telegraph," or the "Times," with the epithet "Capitalist" put after them in brackets. I thought, then, it was the giving of an abnormal epithet to a normal thing; but I now know that these small Socialist free papers were talking the plainest common sense when they specifically emphasized as Capitalist the falsehoods and suppressions of their great contemporaries. From the Socialist point of view the leading fact about the insincerity of the great official papers is that this insincerity is Capitalist; just as from a Catholic point of view the leading fact about it was, and is, that it is anti-Catholic.

Though, however, certain of the Socialist Free Papers thus boldly took up a standpoint of moral equality with the others, their attitude was exceptional. Most editors or owners of, most writers upon, the Free Press, in its first beginnings, took the then almost universal point of view that the great papers were innocuous enough and fairly represented general opinion, and were, therefore, not things to be specifically combated.

The great Dailies were thought grey; not wicked—only general and vague. The Free Press in its beginnings did not attack as an enemy. It only timidly claimed to be heard. It regarded itself as a "speciality." It was humble. And there went with it a mass of excentric stuff.

If one passes in review all the Free Press journals which owed their existence in England and France alone to this motive of Propaganda, one finds many "side shows," as it were, beside the main motives of local or race patriotism, Religion, or Socialist conviction. You have, for instance, up and down Europe, the very powerful and exceedingly well-written anti-Semitic papers, of which Drumont's "Libre Parole" was long the chief. You have the Single-tax papers. You have the Teetotal papers—and, really, it is a wonder that you have not yet also had the Iconoclasts and the Diabolists producing papers. The Rationalist and the Atheist propaganda I reckon among the religious.

We may take it, then, that Propaganda was, in order of time, the first motive of the Free Press and the first cause of its production.

Now from this fact arises a consideration of great importance to our subject. This Propagandist origin of the Free Press stamped it from its outset with a character it still bears, and will continue to

24

bear, until it has had that effect in correcting, and, perhaps, destroying, the Official Press, to which I shall later turn.

I mean that the Free Press has had stamped upon it the character of disparate particularism.

Wherever I go, my first object, if I wish to find out the truth, is to get hold of the Free Press in France as in England, and even in America. But I know that wherever I get hold of such an organ it will be very strongly coloured with the opinion, or even fanaticism, of some minority. The Free Press, as a whole, if you add it all up and cancel out one exaggerated statement against another, does give you a true view of the state of society in which you live. The Official Press to-day gives you an absurdly false one everywhere. What a caricature—and what a base, empty caricature—of England or France or Italy you get in the "Times," or the "Manchester Guardian," the "Matin," or the "Tribune"! No one of them is in any sense general—or really national.

The Free Press gives you the truth; but only in disjointed sections, for it is disparate and it is particularist: it is marked with isolation—and it is so marked because its origin lay in various and most diverse propaganda: because it came later than the official Press of Capitalism, and was, in its origins, but a reaction against it.


**B**


The second motive, that of indignation against falsehood, came to work much later than the motive of propaganda.

Men gradually came to notice that one thing after another of great public interest, sometimes of vital public interest, was deliberately suppressed in the principal great official papers, and that positive falsehoods were increasingly suggested, or stated.

There was more than this. For long the owner of a newspaper had for the most part been content to regard it as a revenue-producing thing. The editor was supreme in matters of culture and opinion. True, the editor, being revocable and poor, could not pretend to full political power. But it was a sort of dual arrangement which yet modified the power of the vulgar owner.

I myself remember that state of affairs: the editor who was a gentleman and dined out, the proprietor who was a lord and nervous when he met a gentleman. It changed in the nineties of the last century or the late eighties. It had disappeared by the 1900's.

The editor became (and now is) a mere mouthpiece of the proprietor. Editors succeed each other rapidly. Of great papers to-day the editor's name of the moment is hardly known—but not a

Cabinet Minister that could not pass an examination in the life, vices, vulnerability, fortune, investments and favours of the owner. The change was rapidly admitted. It came quickly but thoroughly. At last—like most rapid developments—it exceeded itself.

Men owning the chief newspapers could be heard boasting of their power in public, as an admitted thing; and as this power was recognized, and as it grew with time and experiment, it bred a reaction.

Why should this or that vulgarian (men began to say) exercise (and boast of!) the power to keep the people ignorant upon matters vital to us all? To distort, to lie? The sheer necessity of getting certain truths told, which these powerful but hidden fellows refused to tell, was a force working at high potential and almost compelling the production of Free Papers side by side with the big Official ones. That is why you nearly always find the Free Press directed by men of intelligence and cultivation—of exceptional intelligence and cultivation. And that is where it contrasts most with its opponents.

## C

But only a little later than this second motive of indignation against falsehood and acting with equal force (though upon fewer men) was the third motive of freedom: of indignation against arbitrary Power.

For men who knew the way in which we are governed, and who recognized, especially during the last twenty years, that the great newspaper was coming to be more powerful than the open and responsible (though corrupt) Executive of the country, the position was intolerable.

It is bad enough to be governed by an aristocracy or a monarch whose executive power is dependent upon legend in the mass of the people; it is humiliating enough to be thus governed through a sort of play-acting instead of enjoying the self-government of free men.

It is worse far to be governed by a clique of Professional Politicians bamboozling the multitude with a pretence of "Democracy."

But it is intolerable that similar power should reside in the hands of obscure nobodies about whom no illusion could possibly exist, whose tyranny is not admitted or public at all, who do not even take the risk of exposing their features, and to whom no responsibility whatever attaches.

The knowledge that this was so provided the third, and, perhaps, the most powerful motive for the creation of a Free Press.

Unfortunately, it could affect only very few men. With the mass even of well-educated and observant men the feeling created by the novel power of the great papers was little more than a vague ill ease. They had a general conception that the owner of a widely circulated popular newspaper could, and did, blackmail the professional politician: make or unmake the professional politician by granting or refusing him the limelight; dispose of Cabinets; nominate absurd Ministers.

But the particular, vivid, concrete instances that specially move men to action were hidden from them. Only a small number of people were acquainted with such particular truths. But that small number knew very well that we were thus in reality governed by men responsible to no one, and hidden from public blame. The determination to be rid of such a secret monopoly of power compelled a reaction: and that reaction was the Free Press.

# XII

Such being the motive powers of the Free Press in all countries, but particularly in France and England, where the evils of the Capitalist (or Official) Press were at their worst, let us next consider the disabilities under which this reaction—the Free Press—suffered.

I think these disabilities lie under four groups.

(1) In the first place, the free journals suffered from the difficulty which all true reformers have, that they have to begin by going against the stream.

(2) In the second place they suffered from that character of particularism or "crankiness," which was a necessary result of their Propagandist character.

(3) In the third place—and this is most important—they suffered economically. They were unable to present to their readers all that their readers expected at the price. This was because they were refused advertisement subsidy and were boycotted.

(4) In the fourth place, for reasons that will be apparent in a moment, they suffered from lack of information.

To these four main disabilities the Free Papers in this country added a fifth peculiarly our own; they stood in peril from the arbitrary power of the Political Lawyers.

Let us consider first the main four points. When we have

examined them all we shall see against what forces, and in spite of what negative factors, the Free Press has established itself to-day.

## 1

I say that in the first place the Free Press, being a reformer, suffered from what all reformers suffer from, to wit, that in their origins they must, by definition, go against the stream.

The official Capitalist Press round about them had already become a habit when the Free Papers appeared. Men had for some time made it a normal thing to read their daily paper; to believe what it told them to be facts, and even in a great measure to accept its opinion. A new voice criticizing by implication, or directly blaming or ridiculing a habit so formed, was necessarily an unpopular voice with the mass of readers, or, if it was not unpopular, that was only because it was negligible.

This first disability, however, under which the Free Press suffered, and still suffers, would not naturally have been of long duration. The remaining three were far graver. For the mere inertia or counter current against which any reformer struggles is soon turned if the reformer (as was the case here) represented a real reaction, and was doing or saying things which the people, had they been as well informed as himself, would have agreed with. With the further disabilities of (2) particularism, (3) poverty, (4) insufficiency (to which I add, in this country, restraint by the political lawyers), it was otherwise.

## 2

The Particularism of the Free Papers was a grave and permanent weakness which still endures. Any instructed man to-day who really wants to find out what is going on reads the Free Press; but he is compelled, as I have said, to read the whole of it and piece together the sections if he wishes to discover his true whereabouts. Each particular organ gives him an individual impression, which is ex-centric, often highly ex-centric, to the general impression.

When I want to know, for instance, what is happening in France, I read the Jewish Socialist paper, the "Humanité"; the most violent French Revolutionary papers I can get, such as "La Guerre Sociale"; the Royalist "Action Française"; the anti-Semitic "Libre Parole," and so forth.

If I want to find out what is really happening with regard to Ireland, I not only buy the various small Irish free papers (and they are numerous), but also "The New Age" and the "New Witness": and so on, all through the questions that are of real and vital interest. But I only get my picture as a composite. The very same truth will be emphasized by different Free Papers for totally different motives.

Take the Marconi case. The big official papers first boycotted it for months, and then told a pack of silly lies in support of the politicians. The Free Press gave one the truth but its various organs gave the truth for very different reasons and with very different impressions. To some of the Irish papers Marconi was a comic episode, "just what one expects of Westminster"; others dreaded it for fear it should lower the value of the Irish-owned Marconi shares. "The New Age" looked at it from quite another point of view than that of the "New Witness," and the specifically Socialist Free Press pointed it out as no more than an example of what happens under Capitalist Government.

A Mahommedan paper would no doubt have called it a result of the Nazarene religion, and a Thug paper an awful example of what happens when your politicians are not Thugs.

My point is, then, that the Free Press thus starting from so many different particular standpoints has not yet produced a general organ; by which I mean that it has not produced an organ such as would command the agreement of a very great body of men, should that very great body of men be instructed on the real way in which we are governed.

Drumont was very useful for telling one innumerable particular fragments of truth, which the Official Press refuse to mention—such as the way in which the Rothschilds cheated the French Government over the death duties in Paris some years ago. Indeed, he alone ultimately compelled those wealthy men to disgorge, and it was a fine piece of work. But when he went on to argue that cheating the revenue was a purely Jewish vice he could never get the mass of people to agree with him, for it was nonsense.

Charles Maurras is one of the most powerful writers living, and when he points out in the "Action Française" that the French Supreme Court committed an illegal action at the close of the Dreyfus case, he is doing useful work, for he is telling the truth on a matter of vital public importance. But when he goes on to say that such a thing would not have occurred under a nominal Monarchy, he is talking nonsense. Any one with the slightest experience of what the Courts of Law can be under a nominal Monarchy shrugs his shoulders and says that Maurras's action may have excellent results, but that his proposed remedy of setting up one of these modern Kingships in. France in the place of the very corrupt Parliament is not convincing.

The "New Republic" in New York vigorously defends Brandeis because Brandeis is a Jew, and the "New Republic" (which I read regularly, and which is invaluable to-day as an independent instructor on a small rich minority of American opinion) is Jewish in tone. The defence of Brandeis interests me and instructs me. But when the "New Republic" prints pacifist propaganda by Brailsford, or applauds Lane under the alias of "Norman Angell," it is—in my view—eccentric and even contemptible. "New Ireland" helps me to understand the quarrel of the younger men in Ireland with the Irish Parliamentary party—but I must, and do, read the "Freeman" as well.

In a word, the Free Press all over the world, as far as I can read it, suffers from this note of particularity, and, therefore, of isolation and strain. It is not of general appeal.

In connection with this disability you get the fact that the Free Press has come to depend upon individuals, and thus fails to be as yet an institution. It is difficult, to see how any of the papers I have named would long survive a loss of their present editorship. There might possibly be one successor; there certainly would not be two; and the result is that the effect of these organs is sporadic and irregular.

In the same connection you have the disability of a restricted audience.

There are some men (and I count myself one) who will read anything, however much they differ from its tone and standpoint, in order to obtain more knowledge. I am not sure that it is a healthy habit. At any rate it is an unusual one. Most men will only read that which, while informing them, takes for granted a philosophy more or less sympathetic with their own. The Free Press, therefore, so long as it springs from many and varied minorities, not only suffers everywhere from an audience restricted in the case of each organ, but from preaching to the converted. It does get hold of a certain outside public which increases slowly, but it captures no great area of public attention at any one time.

**3**

The third group of disabilities, as I have said, attaches to the economic weakness of the Free Press.

The Free Press is rigorously boycotted by the great advertisers, partly, perhaps, because its small circulation renders

30

them contemptuous (because nearly all of them are of the true wooden-headed "business" type that go in herds and never see for themselves where their goods will find the best market); but much more from frank enmity against the existence of any Free Press at all.

Stupidity, for instance, would account for the great advertisers not advertising articles of luxury in a paper with only a three thousand a week circulation, even if that paper were read from cover to cover by all the rich people in England; but it would not account for absence in the Free Press alone of advertisements appearing in every other kind of paper, and in many organs of far smaller circulation than the Free Press papers have.

The boycott is deliberate, and is persistently maintained. The effect is that the Free Press cannot give in space and quality of paper, excellence of distribution, and the rest, what the Official Press can give; for it lacks advertisement subsidy. This is a very grave economic handicap indeed.

In part the Free Press is indirectly supported by a subsidy from its own writers. Men whose writing commands high payment will contribute to the Free Press sometimes for small fees, usually for nothing; but, at any rate, always well below their market prices. But contribution of that kind is always precarious, and, if I may use the word, jerky. Meanwhile, it does not fill a paper. It is true that the level of writing in the Free Press is very much higher than in the Official Press. To compare the Notes in "The New Age," for instance, with the Notes in the "Spectator" is to discern a contrast like that between one's chosen conversation with equals, and one's forced conversation with commercial travellers in a rail-way carriage. To read Shaw or Wells or Gilbert or Cecil Chesterton or Quiller Couch or any one of twenty others in the "New Witness" is to be in another world from the sludge and grind of the official weekly. But the boycott is rigid and therefore the supply is intermittent. It is not only a boycott of advertisement: it is a boycott of quotation. Most of the governing class know the Free Press. The vast lower middle class does not yet know that it exists.

The occasional articles in the Free Press have the same mark of high value, but it is not regular: and, meanwhile, hardly one of the Free Papers pays its way.

The difficulty of distribution, which I have mentioned, comes under the same heading, and is another grave handicap.

If a man finds a difficulty in getting some paper to which he is not a regular subscriber, but which he desires to purchase more or less regularly, it drops out of his habits. I myself, who am an assiduous reader of all such matter, have sometimes lost touch with one Free Paper or another for months, on account of a couple of weeks' difficulty in getting my copy, I believe this impediment of habit to apply to most of the Free Papers.

# 4

Fourthly, but also partly economic, there is the impediment the Free Press suffers of imperfect information. It will print truths which the Great Papers studiously conceal, but daily and widespread information on general matters it has great difficulty in obtaining.

Information is obtained either at great expense through private agents, or else by favour through official channels, that is, from the professional politicians. The Official Press makes and unmakes the politicians. Therefore, the politician is careful to keep it informed of truths that are valuable to him, as well as to make it the organ of falsehoods equally valuable.

Most of the official papers, for instance, were informed of the Indian Silver scandal by the culprits themselves in a fashion which forestalled attack. Those who led the attack groped in the dark.

For we must remember that the professional politicians all stand in together when a financial swindle is being carried out. There is no "opposition" in these things. Since it is the very business of the Free Press to expose the falsehood or inanity of the Official Capitalist Press, one may truly say that a great part of the energies of the Free Press is wasted in this "groping in the dark" to which it is condemned. At the same time, the Economic difficulty prevents the Free Press from paying for information difficult to be obtained, and under these twin disabilities it remains heavily handicapped.

## The Political Lawyers

We must consider separately, for it is not universal but peculiar to our own society, the heavy disability under which the Free Press suffers in this country from the now unchecked power of the political lawyers.

I have no need to emphasize the power of a Guild when it is once formed, and has behind it strong corporate traditions. It is the principal thesis of "The New Age," in which this essay first appeared, that national guilds, applied to the whole field of society, would be the saving of it through their inherent strength and vitality.

Such guilds as we still have among us (possessed of a Charter

32

giving them a monopoly, and, therefore, making them in "The New Age" phrase "black-leg proof") are confined, of course, to the privileged wealthier classes. The two great ones with which we are all familiar are those of the Doctors and of the Lawyers.

What their power is we saw in the sentencing to one of the most terrible punishments known to all civilized Europe—twelve months hard labour—of a man who had exercised his supposed right to give medical advice to a patient who had freely consulted him. The patient happened to die, as she might have died in the hands of a regular Guild doctor. It has been known for patients to die under the hands of regular Guild doctors. But the mishap taking place in the hands of some one who was not of the Guild, although the advice had been freely sought and honestly given, the person who infringed the monopoly of the Guild suffered this savage piece of revenge.

But even the Guild of the Doctors is not so powerful as that of the Lawyers, qua guild alone. Its administrative power makes it far more powerful. The well-to-do are not compelled to employ a doctor, but all are compelled to employ a lawyer at every turn, and that at a cost quite unknown anywhere else in Europe. But this power of the legal guild, qua guild, in modern England is supplemented by further administrative and arbitrary powers attached to a selected number of its members.

Now the Lawyers' Guild has latterly become (to its own hurt as it will find) hardly distinguishable from the complex of professional politics.

One need not be in Parliament many days to discover that most laws are made and all revised by members of this Guild. Parliament is, as a drafting body, virtually a Committee of Lawyers who are indifferent to the figment of representation which still clings to the House of Commons.

It should be added that this part of their work is honestly done, that the greatest labour is devoted to it, and that it is only consciously tyrannical or fraudulent when the Legal Guild feels itself to be in danger.

But far more important than the legislative power of the Legal Guild (which is now the chief framer of statutory law as it has long been the salutary source of common law) is its executive or governing power.

Whether after exposing a political scandal you shall or shall not be subject to the risk of ruin or loss of liberty, and all the exceptionally cruel scheme of modern imprisonment, depends negatively upon the Legal Guild. That is, so long as the lawyers support the politicians you have no redress, and only in case of independent action by the lawyers against the politicians, with whom they have come to be so closely identified, have you any opportunity for discussion and free trial. The old idea of the lawyer on the Bench protecting the subject against the arbitrary power of the executive, of the judge independent of the government, has nearly disappeared.

You may, of course, commit any crime with impunity if the professional politicians among the lawyers refuse to prosecute. But that is only a negative evil. More serious is the positive side of the affair: that you may conversely be put at the risk of any penalty if they desire to put you at that risk; for the modern secret police being ubiquitous and privileged, their opponent can be decoyed into peril at the will of those who govern, even where the politicians dare not prosecute him for exposing corruption.

Once the citizen has been put at this peril—that is, brought into court before the lawyers—whether it shall lead to his actual ruin or no is again in the hands of members of the legal guild; the judge may (it has happened), withstand the politicians (by whom he was made, to whom he often belongs, and upon whom his general position to-day depends). He may stand out, or—as nearly always now—he will identify himself with the political system and act as its mouthpiece.

It is the prevalence of this last attitude which so powerfully affects the position of the Free Press in this country.

When the judge lends himself to the politicians we all know what follows.

The instrument used is that of an accusation of libel, and, in cases where it is desired to establish terror, of criminal libel.

The defence of the man so accused must either be undertaken by a Member of the Legal Guild—in which case the advocate's own future depends upon his supporting the interests of the politicians and so betraying his client—or, if some eccentric undertakes his own defence, the whole power of the Guild will be turned against him under forms of liberty which are no longer even hypocritical. A special juryman, for instance, that should stand out against the political verdict desired would be a marked man. But the point is not worth making, for, as a fact, no juryman ever has stood out lately when a political verdict was ordered.

Even in the case of so glaring an abuse, with which the whole country is now familiar, we must not exaggerate. It would still be impossible for the politicians, for instance, to get a verdict during war in favour of an overt act of treason. But after all, argument of this sort applies to any tyranny, and the power the politicians have and exercise of refusing to prosecute, however clear an act of treason or other grossly unpopular act might be, is equivalent to a power of acquittal.

The lawyers decide in the last resort on the freedom of speech and writing among their fellow-citizens, and as their Guild is now unhappily intertwined with the whole machinery of Executive Government, we have in modern England an executive controlling the expression of opinion. It is absolute in a degree unknown, I think, in past society.

Now, it is evident that, of all forms of civic activity, writing upon the Free Press most directly challenges this arbitrary power. There is not an editor responsible for the management of any Free Paper who will not tell you that a thousand times he has had to consider whether it were possible to tell a particular truth, however important that truth might be to the commonwealth. And the fear which restrains him is the fear of destruction which the combination of the professional politician, and lawyer holds in its hand. There is not one such editor who could not bear witness to the numerous occasions on which he had, however courageous he might be, to forgo the telling of a truth which was of vital value, because its publication would involve the destruction of the paper he precariously controlled.

There is no need to labour all this. The loss of freedom we have gradually suffered is quite familiar to all of us, and it is among the worst of all the mortal symptoms with which our society is affected.

# XIII

Why do I say, then, that in spite of such formidable obstacles, both in its own character and in the resistance it must overcome, the Free Press will probably increase in power, and may, in the long run, transform public opinion?

It is with the argument in favour of this judgment that I will conclude.

My reasons for forming this judgment are based not only upon the observation of others but upon my own experience.

I started the "Eye-Witness" (succeeded by the "New Witness" under the editorship of Mr. Cecil Chesterton, who took it over from me some years ago, and now under the editorship of his brother, Mr. Gilbert Chesterton) with the special object of providing a new organ of free expression.

I knew from intimate personal experience exactly how formidable all these obstacles were.

I knew how my own paper could not but appear particular and personal, and could not but suffer from that eccentricity to general opinion of which I have spoken. I had a half-tragic and half-comic experience of the economic difficulty; of the difficulty of obtaining information; of the difficulty in distribution, and all the rest of it. The editor of "The New Age" could provide an exactly similar record. I had experience, and after me Mr. Cecil Chesterton had experience, of the threats levelled by the professional politicians and their modern lawyers against the free expression of truth, and I have no doubt that the editor of "The New Age" could provide similar testimony. As for the Free Press in Ireland, we all know how that is dealt with. It is simply suppressed at the will of the police.

In the face of such experience, and in spite of it, I am yet of the deliberate opinion that the Free Press will succeed.

Now let me give my reasons for this audacious conclusion.

# XIV

The first thing to note is that the Free Press is not read perfunctorily, but with close attention. The audience it has, if small, is an audience which never misses its pronouncements whether it agrees or disagrees with them, and which is absorbed in its opinions, its statement of fact and its arguments. Look narrowly at History and you will find that all great reforms have started thus: not through a widespread control acting downwards, but through spontaneous energy, local and intensive, acting upwards.

You cannot say this of the Official Press, for the simple reason that the Official Press is only of real political interest on rare and brief occasions. It is read of course, by a thousand times more people than those who read the Free Press. But its readers are not gripped by it. They are not, save upon the rare occasions of a particular "scoop" or "boom," informed by it, in the old sense of that pregnant word, informed:—they are not possessed, filled, changed, moulded to new action.

One of the proofs of this—a curious, a comic, but a most conclusive proof—is the dependence of the great daily papers on the headline. Ninety-nine people out of a hundred retain this and nothing more, because the matter below is but a flaccid expansion of the headline.

Now the Headline suggests, of course, a fact (or falsehood) with momentary power. So does the Poster. But the mere fact of dependence on such methods is a proof of the inherent weakness underlying it.

36

You have, then, at the outset a difference of quality in the reading and in the effect of the reading which it is of capital importance to my argument that the reader should note. The Free Press is really read and digested. The Official Press is not. Its scream is heard, but it provides no food for the mind. One does not contrast the exiguity of a pint of nitric acid in an engraver's studio with the hundreds of gallons of water in the cisterns of his house. No amount of water would bite into the copper. Only the acid does that: and a little of the acid is enough.

## XV

Next let it be noted that the Free Press powerfully affects, even when they disagree with it, and most of all when they hate it, the small class through whom in the modern world ideas spread.

There never was a time in European history when the mass of people thought so little for themselves, and depended so much (for the ultimate form of their society) upon the conclusions and vocabulary of a restricted leisured body.

That is a diseased state of affairs. It gives all their power to tiny cliques of well-to-do people. But incidentally it helps the Free Press.

It is a restricted leisured body to which the Free Press appeals. So strict has been the boycott—and still is, though a little weakening—that the editors of, and writers upon, the Free Papers probably underestimate their own effect even now. They are never mentioned in the great daily journals. It is a point of honour with the Official Press to turn a phrase upside down, or, if they must quote, to quote in the most roundabout fashion, rather than print in plain black and white the three words "The New Age" or "The New Witness."

But there are a number of tests which show how deeply the effect of a Free Paper of limited circulation bites in. Here is one apparently superficial test, but a test to which I attach great importance because it is a revelation of how minds work. Certain phrases peculiar to the Free Journals find their way into the writing of all the rest. I could give a number of instances. I will give one: the word "profiteer." It was first used in the columns of "The New Age," if I am not mistaken. It has gained ground everywhere. This does not mean that the mass of the employees upon daily papers understand what they are talking about when they use the word "profiteer," any more than they understand what they are talking

37

about when they use the words "servile state." They commonly debase the word "profiteer" to mean some one who gets an exceptional profit, just as they use my own "Eye-Witness" phrase, "The Servile State," to mean strict regulation of all civic life—an idea twenty miles away from the proper signification of the term. But my point is that the Free Press must have had already a profound effect for its mere vocabulary to have sunk in thus, and to have spread so widely in the face of the rigid boycott to which it is subjected.

# XVI

Much more important than this clearly applicable test of vocabulary is the more general and less measurable test of programmes and news. The programme of National Guilds, for instance—"Guild Socialism" as "The New Age," its advocate in this country, has called it—is followed everywhere, and is everywhere considered. Journalists employed by Harmsworth, for instance, use the idea for all it is worth, and they use it more and more, although it is as much as their place is worth to mention "The New Age" in connection with it—as yet. And it is the same, I think, with all the efforts the Free Press has made in the past. The propaganda of Socialism (which, as an idea, was so enormously successful until a few years ago) was, on its journalistic side, almost entirely conducted by Free Papers, most of them of small circulation, and all of them boycotted, even as to their names, by the Official Press. The same is true of my own effort and Mr. Chesterton's on the "New Witness." The paper was rigidly boycotted and never quoted. But every one to-day talks, as I have just said, of "The Servile State," of the "Professional Politician," of the "Secret Party Funds," of the Aliases under which men hide, of the Purchase of Honours, Policies and places in the Government, etc., etc.

More than this: one gets to hear of significant manœuvres, conducted secretly, of course, but showing vividly the weight and effect of the Free Press. One hears of orders given by a politician which prove his fear of the Free Press: of approaches made by this or that Capitalist to obtain control of a free journal: sometimes of a policy initiated, an official document drawn up, a memorandum filed, which proceeded directly from the advice, suggestion, or argument of a Free Paper which no one but its own readers is allowed to hear of, and of whose very existence the suburbs would be sceptical.

Latterly I have noticed something still more significant. The action of the Free Press takes effect sometimes at once. It was obvious in the case of the Spanish Jew Vigo, the German agent. On account of his financial connections all the Official Press had orders to call him French under a false name. One paragraph in the "New Witness" broke down that lie before the week was out.

# XVII

Next consider this powerful factor in the business. The truth confirms itself.

Half a million people read of a professional politician, for instance, that his oratory has an "electric effect," or that he is "full of personal magnetism," or that he "can sway an audience to tears or laughter at will." A Free Paper telling the truth about him says that he is a dull speaker, full of commonplaces, elderly, smelling strongly of the Chapel, and giving the impression that he is tired out; flogging up sham enthusiasm with stale phrases which the reporters have already learnt to put into shorthand with one conventional outline years ago.[1]

Well, the false, the ludicrously false picture designed to put this politician in the limelight (as against favours to be rendered), no doubt remains the general impression with most of those 500,000 people. The simple and rather tawdry truth may be but doubtfully accepted by a few hundreds only.

But sooner or later a certain small proportion of the 500,000 actually hear the politician in question. They hear him speak. They receive a primary and true impression.

If they had not read anything suggesting the truth, it is quite upon the cards that the false suggestion would still have weight with them, in spite of the evidence of their senses. Men are so built that uncontradicted falsehood sufficiently repeated does have that curious power of illusion. A man having heard the speech delivered by the old gentleman, if there were nothing but the Official Press to inform opinion, might go away saying to himself: "I was not very much impressed, but no doubt that was due to my own weariness. I cannot but believe that the general reputation he bears is well founded. He must be a great orator, for I have always heard him called one."

---

[1] A friend of mine in the Press Gallery used to represent "I have yet to learn that the Government" by a little twirl, and "What did the right honourable gentleman do, Mr. Speaker? He had the audacity" by two spiral dots.

But a man who has even once seen it stated that this politician was exactly what he was will vividly remember that description (which at first hearing he probably thought false); physical experience has confirmed the true statement and made it live. These statements of truth, even when they are quite unimportant, more, of course, when they illuminate matters of great civic moment, have a cumulative effect.

I am confident, for instance, that at the present time the mass of middle-class people are not only acquainted with, but convinced of, the truth, that, long before the war, the House of Commons had become a fraud; that its debates did not turn upon matters which really divided opinion, and that even its paltry debating points, the pretence of a true opposition was a falsehood.

This salutary truth had been arrived at, of course, by many other channels. The scandalous arrangement between the Front Benches which forced the Insurance Act down our throats was an eye-opener for the great masses of the people. So was the cynical action of the politicians in the matter of Chinese Labour after the Election of 1906. So was the puerile stage play indulged in over things like the Welsh Disestablishment Bill and the Education Bills.

But among the forces which opened people's eyes about the House of Commons, the Free Press played a very great part, though it was never mentioned in the big Official papers, and though not one man in many hundreds of the public ever heard of it. The few who read it were startled into acceptance by the exact correspondence between its statement and observed fact.

The man who tells the truth when his colleagues around him are lying, always enjoys a certain restricted power of prophecy. If there were a general conspiracy to maintain the falsehood that all peers were over six foot high, a man desiring to correct this falsehood would be perfectly safe if he were to say: "I do not know whether the next peer you meet will be over six foot or not, but I am pretty safe in prophesying that you will find, among the next dozen three or four peers less than six foot high."

If there were a general conspiracy to pretend that people with incomes above the income-tax level never cheated one in a bargain, one could not say "on such-and-such a day you will be cheated in a bargain by such-and-such a person, whose income will be above the income-tax level," but one could say; "Note the people who swindle you in the next five years, and I will prophesy that some of the number will be people paying income-tax."

This power of prophecy, which is an adjunct of truth telling, I have noticed to affect people very profoundly.

40

A worthy provincial might have been shocked ten years ago to hear that places in the Upper House of Parliament were regularly bought and sold. He might have indignantly denied it The Free Press said: "In some short while you will have a glaring instance of a man who is incompetent and obscure but very rich, appearing as a legislator with permanent hereditary power, transferable to his son after his death. I don't know which the next one will be, but there is bound to be a case of the sort quite soon for the thing goes on continually. You will be puzzled to explain it. The explanation is that the rich man has given a large sum of money to the needy professional politician, Selah."

Our worthy provincial may have heard but an echo of this truth, for it would have had, ten years ago, but few readers. He may not have seen a syllable of it in his daily paper. But things happen. He sees first a great soldier, then a well-advertised politician, not a rich man, but very widely talked about, made peers. The events are normal in each case, and he is not moved. But sooner or later there comes a case in which he has local knowledge. He says to himself: "Why on earth is So-and-so made a peer (or a front bench man, or what not)? Why, in the name of goodness, is this very rich but unknown, and to my knowledge incompetent, man suddenly put into such a position?" Then he remembers what he was told, begins to ask questions, and finds out, of course, that money passed; perhaps, if he is lucky, he finds out which professional politician pouched the money—and even how much he took!

# XVIII

The effect of the Free Press from all these causes may be compared to the cumulative effect of one of the great offensives of the present war. Each individual blow is neither dramatic nor extensive in effect; there is little movement or none. The map is disappointing. But each blow tells, and when the end comes every one will see suddenly what the cumulative effect was.

There is not a single thing which the Free Papers have earnestly said during the last few years which has not been borne out by events—and sometimes borne out with astonishing rapidity and identity of detail.

It would, perhaps, be superstitious to believe that strong and courageous truth-telling calls down from Heaven, new, unexpected, and vivid examples to support it. But, really, the events of the last few years would almost incline one to that superstition. The Free

Press has hardly to point out some political truth which the Official Press has refused to publish, when the stars in their courses seem to fight for that truth. It is thrust into the public gaze by some abnormal accident immediately after! Hardly had Mr. Chesterton and I begun to publish articles on the state of affairs at Westminster when the Marconi men very kindly obliged us.

## XIX

But there is a last factor in this progressive advance of the free Press towards success which I think the most important of all. It is the factor of time in the process of human generations.

It is an old tag that the paradox of one age is the commonplace of the next, and that tag is true. It is true, because young men are doubly formed. First, by the reality and freshness of their own experience, and next, by the authority of their elders.

You see the thing in the reputation of poets. For instance, when A is 20, B 40, and C 60, a new poet appears, and is, perhaps, thought an eccentric. "A" cannot help recognizing the new note and admiring it, but he is a little ashamed of what may turn out to be an immature opinion, and he holds his tongue, "B" is too busy in middle life and already too hardened to feel the force of the new note and the authority he has over "A" renders "A" still more doubtful of his own judgment. "C" is frankly contemptuous of the new note. He has sunk into the groove of old age.

Now let twenty years pass, and things will have changed in this fashion. "C" is dead. "B" has grown old, and is of less effect as an authority. "A" is himself in middle age, and is sure of his own taste and not prepared to take that of elders. He has already long expressed his admiration for the new poet, who is, indeed, not a "new poet" any longer, but, perhaps, already an established classic.

We are all witnesses to this phenomenon in the realm of literature. I believe that the same thing goes on with even more force in the realm of political ideas.

Can any one conceive the men who were just leaving the University five or six years ago returning from the war and still taking the House of Commons seriously? I cannot conceive it. As undergraduates they would already have heard of its breakdown; as young men they knew that the expression of this truth was annoying to their elders, and they always felt when they expressed it—perhaps they enjoyed feeling—that there was something impertinent and odd, and possibly exaggerated in their attitude. But when they are

42

men between 30 and 40 they will take so simple a truth for granted. There will be no elders for them to fear, and they will be in no doubt upon judgments maturely formed. Unless something like a revolution occurs in the habits and personal constitution of the House of Commons it will by that time be a joke and let us hope already a partly innocuous joke.

With this increasing and cumulative effect of truth-telling, even when that truth is marred or distorted by enthusiasm, all the disabilities under which it has suffered will coincidently weaken. The strongest force of all against people's hearing the truth—the arbitrary power still used by the political lawyers to suppress Free writing—will, I think, weaken.

The Courts, after all, depend largely upon the mass of opinion. Twenty years ago, for instance, an accusation of bribery brought against some professional politician would have been thought a monstrosity, and, however true, would nearly always have given the political lawyers, his colleagues, occasion for violent repression. To-day the thing has become so much a commonplace that all appeals to the old illusion would fall flat. The presiding lawyer could not put on an air of shocked incredulity at hearing that such-and-such a Minister had been mixed up in such-and-such a financial scandal. We take such things for granted nowadays.

## XX

What I do doubt in the approaching and already apparent success of the Free Press is its power to effect democratic reform.

It will succeed at last in getting the truth told pretty openly and pretty thoroughly. It will break down the barrier between the little governing clique in which the truth is cynically admitted and the bulk of educated men and women who cannot get the truth by word of mouth but depend upon the printed word. We shall, I believe, even within the lifetime of those who have taken part in the struggle; have all the great problems of our time, particularly the Economic problems, honestly debated. But what I do not see is the avenue whereby the great mass of the people can now be restored to an interest in the way in which they are governed, or even in the re-establishment of their own economic independence.

So far as I can gather from the life around me, the popular appetite for freedom and even for criticism has disappeared. The wage-earner demands sufficient and regular subsistence, including a system of pensions, and, as part of his definition of subsistence and sufficiency, a due portion of leisure. That he demands a property in the means of production, I can see no sign whatever. It may come; but all the evidence is the other way. And as for a general public indignation against corrupt government, there is (below the few in the know who either share the swag or shrug their shoulders) no sign that it will be strong enough to have any effect.

All we can hope to do is, for the moment, negative: in my view, at least. We can undermine the power of the Capitalist Press. We can expose it as we have exposed the Politicians. It is very powerful but very vulnerable—as are all human things that repose on a lie. We may expect, in a delay perhaps as brief as that which was required to pillory, and, therefore, to hamstring the miserable falsehood and ineptitude called the Party System (that is, in some ten years or less), to reduce the Official Press to the same plight. In some ways the danger of failure is less, for our opponent is certainly less well-organized. But beyond that—beyond these limits—we shall not attain. We shall enlighten, and by enlightening, destroy. We shall not provoke public action, for the methods and instincts of corporate civic action have disappeared.

Such a conclusion might seem to imply that the deliberate and continued labour of truth-telling without reward, and always in some peril, is useless; and that those who have for now so many years given their best work freely for the establishment of a Free Press have toiled in vain, I intend no such implication: I intend its very opposite.

I shall myself continue in the future, as I have in the past, to write and publish in that Press without regard to the Boycott in publicity and in advertisement subsidy which is intended to destroy it and to make all our effort of no effect. I shall continue to do so, although I know that in "The New Age" or the "New Witness" I have but one reader, where in the "Weekly Dispatch" or the "Times" I should have a thousand.

I shall do so, and the others who continue in like service will do so, first, because, though the work is so far negative only, there is (and we all instinctively feel it), a Vis Medicatrix Naturæ: merely in weakening an evil you may soon be, you ultimately will surely be, creating a good: secondly, because self-respect and honour demand it. No man who has the truth to tell and the power to tell it can long remain hiding it from fear or even from despair without ignominy. To release the truth against whatever odds, even if so doing can no longer help the Commonwealth, is a necessity for the soul.

We have also this last consolation, that those who leave us and attach themselves from fear or greed to the stronger party of dissemblers gradually lose thereby their chance of fame in letters. Sound writing cannot survive in the air of mechanical hypocrisy.

44

They with their enormous modern audiences are the hacks doomed to oblivion. We, under the modern silence, are the inheritors of those who built up the political greatness of England upon a foundation of free speech, and of the prose which it begets. Those who prefer to sell themselves or to be cowed gain, as a rule, not even that ephemeral security for which they betrayed their fellows; meanwhile, they leave to us the only solid and permanent form of political power, which is the gift of mastery through persuasion.

# THE HISTORIC THAMES

England has been built up upon the framework of her rivers, and, in that pattern, the principal line has been the line of the Thames.

Partly because it was the main highway of Southern England, partly because it looked eastward towards the Continent from which the national life has been drawn, partly because it was better served by the tide than any other channel, but mainly because it was the chief among a great number of closely connected river basins, the Thames Valley has in the past supported the government and the wealth of England.

Among the most favoured of our rivals some one river system has developed a province or a series of provinces; the Rhine has done so, the Seine and the Garonne. But the great Continental river systems—at least the navigable ones—stand far apart from one another: in this small, and especially narrow, country of Britain navigable river systems are not only numerous, but packed close together. It is perhaps on this account that we have been under less necessity in the past to develop our canals; and anyone who has explored the English rivers in a light boat knows how short are the portages between one basin and another.

Now not only are we favoured with a multitude of navigable waterways—the tide makes even our small coastal rivers navigable right inland—but also we are quite exceptionally favoured in them when we consider that the country is an island.

If an island, especially an island in a tidal sea, has a good river system, that system is bound to be of more benefit to it than would be a similar system to a Continental country. For it must mean that the tide will penetrate everywhere into the heart of the plains, carrying the burden of their wealth backward and forward, mixing their peoples, and filling the whole national life with its energy; and this will be especially the case in an island which is narrow in proportion to its length and in which the rivers are distributed transversely to its axis.

When we consider the river systems of the other great islands of Europe we find that none besides our own enjoys this advantage. Sicily and Crete, apart from the fact that they do not stand in tidal water, have no navigable rivers. Iceland, standing in a tidal sea, too far north indeed for successful commerce, but not too far north for the growth of a civilisation, is at a similar disadvantage. Great

46

Britain and Ireland alone—Great Britain south of the Scottish Mountains, that is—enjoy this peculiar advantage; and there are few things more instructive when one is engaged upon the history of England than to take a map and mark upon it the head of each navigable piece of water and the head of its tideway, for when this has been done all England, with the exception of the Welsh Hills and the Pennines, seems to be penetrated by the influence of the sea.

The conditions which give a river this great historic importance, the fundamental character, therefore, which has lent to the Thames its meaning in English history, is twofold: a river affords a permanent means of travel, and a river also forms an obstacle and a boundary. Men are known to have agglomerated in the beginning of society in two ways: as nomadic hordes and as fixed inhabitants of settlements.

There has arisen a profitless discussion as to which of these two phases came first. No evidence can possibly exist upon either side, but one may take it that with the first traditions and records, as at the present time, the two systems existed side by side, and that either was determined by geographical conditions. A river is an advantage to both groups, but to the second it is of more consequence than to the first; and in South England, if we go back to the origins of our history, it is in fixed settlements that we find the first evidence of man. With every year of research the extreme antiquity of our inhabited sites becomes more apparent. And indeed the geographical nature of Southern England should make us certain of the antiquity of village life in it, even were there no archæological evidence to support that antiquity.

South England is everywhere fertile, everywhere well watered, and nowhere divided, as is the North, by long districts of bare country, or of hills snowbound in winter, or of morass. Its forests, though numerous, have never formed one continuous belt; even the largest of them, the Forest of the Weald, between the downs of Surrey and Kent and those of Sussex, was but twenty miles across— large enough to nourish a string of hunting villages upon the north and the south edges of it; but not large enough to isolate the Thames Valley from the southern coast.

From the beginning of human activity in this island the whole length of the river has been set with human settlements never far removed one from the other; for the Thames ran through the heart of South England, and wherever its banks were secure from recurrent floods it furnished those who settled on them with three main things which every early village requires: good water, defence, and communication.

The importance of the first lessens as men learn to dig wells and to canalise springs; the two last, defence and communication, remain attached to river settlements to a much later date, and are apparent in all the history of the Thames.

The problem of communication under early conditions is serious. Even in a high civilisation the maintenance of roads is of greater moment, and imposes a greater burden, than most of the citizens who support it know; but before the means or the knowledge exist to survey and to harden roads, with their causeways over marshes and their bridges over rivers, the supply of food in time of scarcity or of succour in time of danger is never secure: a little narrow path kept up by nothing but the continual passage of men and animals is all the channel a community of men have for communicating with their neighbours by land. And it must be remembered that upon such communication depend not only the present existence, but the future development of the society, which cannot proceed except by that fertilisation, as it were, which comes from the mixture of varied experiences and of varied traditions: every great change in history has necessarily been accompanied by some new activity of travel.

Under the primitive conditions of which we speak a river of moderate depth, not too rapid in its current and perennial in its supply, is much the best means by which men may communicate. It will easily carry, by the exertions of a couple of men, some hundred times the weight the same men could have carried as porters by land. It furnishes, if it is broad, a certain security from attack during the journey; it will permit the rapid passage of a large number abreast where the wood tracks and paths of the land compel a long procession; and it furnishes the first of the necessities of life continually as the journey proceeds.

Upon all these accounts a river, during the natural centuries which precede and follow the epochs of high civilisation, is as much more important than the road or the path as, let us say, a railway to-day is more important than a turnpike.

What is equally interesting, when a high civilisation after its little effort begins to decline into one of those long periods of repose into which all such periods of energy do at last decline, the river reassumes its importance. There is a very interesting example of this in the history of France. Before Roman civilisation reached the north of Gaul the Seine and its tributary streams were evidently the chief economic factor in the life of the people: this may be seen in the sites of their strongholds and in the relation of the tribes to one another, as for instance, the dependence of the Parisians upon Sens. The five centuries of active Roman civilisation saw the river replaced by the system of Roman roads; the great artificial track from north to south, for instance, takes on a peculiar importance; but when the end of that period has come, and the energies of the Roman state are beginning to drag, when the money cannot be collected to repair the great highways, and these fall into decay— then the Seine and its tributaries reassume their old importance. Paris, the junction of the various waterways, becomes the capital of a new state, and the influence of its kings leads out upon every side along the river valleys which fall into the main valley of the Seine.

There are but two considerable modifications to the use for habitation of slow and constant rivers: their value is lessened or interrupted by precipitous banks or they are rendered unapproachable by marshes. The first of these causes, for instance, has singularly cut off one from the other the groups of population residing upon the upper and the lower Meuse, as it has also, to quote another example, cut off even in language the upper from the lower Elbe.

From this first species of interruption the Thames is, of course, singularly free. There is no river in England, with the exception of the Trent, whose banks interfere so little with the settlement of men in any place on account of their steepness.

As to the second, the Thames presents a somewhat rare character.

The upper part of the river, which is in lowland valleys the most easily inhabited, and the part in which, once the river is navigable, will be found the largest number of small settlements, is in the case of the Thames the most marshy. From its source to beyond Cricklade the river runs entirely over clay; thenceforward the valley is a flat mass of alluvium, in which the stream swings from one side to the other, and even where it touches higher soil, touches nothing better than the continuation of this clay. In spite, therefore, of the shallowness and narrowness of the upper river there always existed this impediment which an insecure soil would present to the formation of any considerable settlements. The loneliness of the stretch below Kelmscott is due to an original difficulty of this kind, and the one considerable settlement upon the upper river at Lechlade stands upon the only place where firm ground approaches the bank of the river.

This formation endures well below Oxford until one reaches the gap at Sandford, where the stream passes between two beds of gravel which very nearly approach either bank.

Above this point the Thames is everywhere, upon one side or the other, guarded by flat river meadows, which must in early times have been morass; and nowhere were these more difficult of

49

passage than in the last network of streams between Witham Hill and Sandford, to the west of the gravel bank upon which Oxford is built.

Below Sandford, and on all the way to London Bridge, the character of the river in this respect changes. You have everywhere gravel or flinty chalk, with but a narrow bed of alluvial soil, upon either bank to represent the original overflow of the river.

At the crossing places (as we shall see later), notably at Long Wittenham, at Wallingford, at Streatley, at Pangbourne, and, still lower, at Maidenhead and at Ealing, this hard soil came right down to the bank upon either side.

On all this lower half of the Thames marsh was rare, and was to be found even in early times only in isolated patches, which are still clearly defined. These are never found facing each other upon opposite banks of the stream. Thus there was a bad bit on the left bank above Abingdon, but the large marsh below Abingdon, where the Ock came in, was on the right bank, with firm soil opposite it. There was a large bay, as it were, of drowned land on the right bank, from below Reading to a point opposite Shiplake, the last wide morass before the marshes of the tidal portion of the river; and another at the mouth of the Coln, above Staines, on the left bank, which was the last before one came to the mud of the tidal estuary; and even the tidal marshes were fairly firm above London. From Staines eastward down as far as Chelsea the superficial soil upon either side is of gravels, and the long list of ancient inhabited sites upon either bank show how little the overflow of the river interfered with its usefulness to men.

The river, then, from Sandford downward has afforded upon either bank innumerable sites upon which a settlement could be formed. Above Sandford these sites are not to be found indifferently upon either bank, but now on one, now on the other. There is no case on the upper river of two villages facing each other on either side of the stream. But though the soil of this upper part was in general less suited to the establishment of settlements, a certain number of firmer stretches could be found, and advantage was taken of them to build.

There thus arose along the whole course of the Thames from its source to London a series of villages and towns, increasing in importance as the stream deepened and gave greater facilities to traffic, and bound together by the common life of the river. It was their highway, and it is as a highway that it must first be regarded.

Of the way in which the Thames was a necessary great road in early times, perhaps the best proof is the manner in which various parishes manage to get their water front at the expense of a somewhat unnatural shape to their boundaries. Thus Fawley in Buckinghamshire has a curious and interesting arrangement of this sort thrusting down from the hills a tongue of land which ends in a sort of wharfage on the river just opposite Remenham church. In Berkshire there are also several examples of this. On the upper river Dractmoor and Kingston Bagpuise are both very narrow and long, a shape forced upon them by the necessity of having this outlet upon the river in days when the life of a parish was a real one and the village was a true and self-sufficing unit. Next to them Fyfield does the same thing. Lower down, near Wallingford, the parish of Brightwell has added on a similar eccentric edge to the north and east so that it may share in the bank; but perhaps the best example of all in this connection is the curious extension below Reading. Here land which is of no use for human habitation—water meadows continually liable to floods—runs out from the parish northward for a good mile. These lands are separated from the river during the whole of this extension until at last a bend of the stream gives the parish the opportunity it has evidently sought in thus extending its boundaries. On the Oxford bank Standlake and Brighthampton do the same thing upon the Upper Thames and to some extent Eynsham; for when one thinks how far back Eynsham stands from the river it is somewhat remarkable that it should have claimed the right to get at the stream. Below Oxford there is another most interesting instance of the same thing in the case of Littlemore. Littlemore stands on high and dry land up above the river somewhat set back from it. Sandford evidently interfered with its access to the water, and Littlemore has therefore claimed an obviously artificial extension for all the world like a great foot added on to the bulk of the parish. This "foot" includes Kennington Island, and runs up the meadows to the foot of that eyot.

The long and narrow parishes in the reaches below Benson, Nuneham Morren, Mongewell, and Ipsden and South Stoke are not, however, examples of this tendency.

They owe their construction to the same causes as have produced the similar long parishes of the Surrey and the Sussex Weald. The life of the parish was in each case right on the river or very close to it, and the extension is not the attempt of the parish to reach the river, but the claim of the parish upon the hunting lands which lay up behind it upon the Chiltern Hills. The truth of this will be apparent to anyone who notes upon the map the way in which parishes are thus lengthened, not only on the western side of the hills, but also upon the farther eastern side, where there was no connection with the river.

There are many other proofs remaining of the chief function

which the Thames fulfilled in the early part of our history as a means of communication.

We shall see later in these pages how united all that line of the stream has been; how the great monasteries founded upon the Thames were supported by possessions stretched all along the valleys; how much of it, and what important parts, were held by the Crown; and how strong was the architectural influence of towns upon one another up and down the water, as also how the place names upon the banks are everywhere drawn from the river; but before dealing with these it is best to establish the main portions into which the Thames falls and to see what would naturally be their limits.

It may be said, generally, that every river which is tidal, and whose stream is so slow as to be easily navigable in either direction, divides itself naturally, when one is regarding it as a means of communication, into three main divisions.

There will first of all be the tidal portion which the tide usually scours into an estuary. As a general rule, this portion is not considerably inhabited in the early periods of history, for it is not until a large international commerce arises that vessels have much occasion to stop as they pass up and down the maritime part of the stream; and even so, settlements upon its banks must come comparatively late in the development of the history of the river, because a landing upon such flooded banks is not easily to be effected.

This is true of the Dutch marshes at the mouths of the Rhine, whose civilisation (one exclusively due to the energy of man) came centuries after the establishment of the great Roman towns of the Rhine; it is true of the estuary of the Seine, whose principal harbour of Havre is almost modern, and whose difficulties are still formidable for ocean-going craft; and it is true of the Thames.

The estuary of the Thames plays little or no part in the very early history of England. Invaders, when they landed, landed on the sea-coast at the very mouth, or appear to have sailed right up into the heart of the country.

It is, nevertheless, true that the last few miles of tidal water, in Western Europe at least, are not to be included in this first division of a great river.

The swish of the tide continues up beyond the broad estuary, the sand-banks, and the marshes, and there are reaches more or less long (rather less than twenty miles perhaps originally in the case of the Thames, rather more perhaps originally in the case of the lower Seine) which for the purposes of habitation are inland reaches. They have the advantage of a current moving in either direction twice a day and yet not the disadvantage of greatly varying levels of water. Thus one may say of the Seine in the old days that from about Caudebec to Point de L'Arche it enjoyed such inland tidal conditions; and of the Thames from Greenwich to Teddington that similar advantages existed.

The true point of division which separates, so far as human history is concerned, the lower from the upper part of such rivers is the first bridge, and, what almost always accompanies the first bridge, the first great town. To repeat the obvious parallel, Rouen was this point upon the Seine; upon the Thames this point was the Bridge of London. It is with the habitable and historic Thames Valley above the bridge that this book has to deal, and it will later be to the reader's purpose to consider why London Bridge crossed the stream just where it did, and of what moment that site has been in the history of the Thames and of England.

The second division in a great European tidal river, considered as a means of communication, is the navigable but non-tidal portion.

The word navigable is so vague that it requires some definition before we can apply it to any particular stream. It does not, of course, mean in this connection "navigable by sea-going boats." One may take a constant depth of so little as three feet to be sufficient for the purpose of carrying merchandise even in considerable bulk.

The legislatures of various countries have established varying gauges to determine where the navigability of a river may be said to cease. In practice these gauges have always been arbitrary. The upper reaches of a river may present sufficient depth but too fast a current, or they may be too narrow, or the curves may be too rapid, or the obstruction of rocks too common, for any sort of navigation, although the depth of water be sufficient.

Conversely, in some streams of peculiar breadth and constancy very shallow upper reaches may have early been converted to the use of man. The matter is only to be determined by the experience of what the inhabitants of a river valley have actually been able to do under the local circumstances, and when we examine this we shall usually be astonished to see how far inland a river was used until the history of internal navigation was transformed by the development of canals or partially destroyed by the development of railways. Thus it is certain that so small a stream as the Adur in Sussex floated barges up to the boundaries of Shipley Parish; that the Stour was habitually used beyond Canterbury; that so tiny a tributary as the Ant in Norfolk was followed up from its parent Bure to the neighbourhood of Worsted.

53

In this connection the Thames is of an especial interest, for it had, in proportion to its length, the greatest section of navigable non-tidal water of any of the shorter rivers in Europe. Until the digging of the Thames and Severn Canal at the end of last century it was possible, and even common, for boats to reach Cricklade, or at any rate the mouth of the Churn. And even now, in spite of the pumping that is necessary at Thames head and the consequent diminution of the volume of water in the upper reaches, the Thames, were water carriage to come again into general use, would be a busy commercial stream as high up as Lechlade.

This exceptional sector of non-tidal navigable water cutting right across England from east to west, and that in what used to be the most productive and is still the most fertile portion of the island, is the chief factor in the historic importance of the Thames.

From Cricklade to the navigable waters of the Severn Valley is but a long day's walk; and one may say that even in the earliest times there was thus provided a great highway right across what then was by far the most thickly populated and the most important part of the island.

A third section in all such rivers (and, from what we have said above, a short and insignificant one in the case of the Thames) may be called the head-waters of the river: where the stream is so shallow or so uncertain as to be no longer navigable. In the case of the Thames these head-waters cover no more than ten to fifteen miles of country. With the exception of rivers that run through mountain districts this section of a river's course is nearly always small in proportion to the rest; but the Thames, just as it has the longest proportion of navigable water, has also by far the shortest proportion of useless head-water of all the shorter European rivers.

There is a further discussion as to what is the true source of the Thames, and which streams may properly be regarded as its head-waters: the Churn, especially since the digging of the canal, having a larger flow than the stream from Thames head; but whichever is chosen, the non-navigable portion starts at the same point, and is the third of the divisions into which the valley ranges itself when it is considered in its length, as a highway from the west to the east of England. The two limits, then, are at London Bridge and at Cricklade, or rather at some point between Lechlade and Cricklade, and nearer to the latter.

But a river has a second topographical and historic function. It cannot only be considered longitudinally as a highway, it can also be considered in relation to transverse forces and regarded as an obstacle, a defence, and a boundary.

This function has, of course, been of the highest importance in the history of all great rivers, not perhaps so much so in the case of the Thames as in the case of swifter or deeper streams, but, still, more than has been the case with so considerable and so rapid a river as the Po in Lombardy or the uncertain but dangerous Loire in its passage through the centre of France. For the Thames Valley was that which divided the vague Mercian land from which we get our weights, our measures, and the worst of our national accent, and cut it off from that belt of the south country which was the head and the heart of England until the last industrial revolution of our history.

The Thames also has entered to a large, though hardly to a determining, extent into the military history of the country; to an extent which is greater in earlier than in later times, because with every new bridge the military obstacle afforded by the stream diminished. And finally, the Thames, regarded as an obstacle, was the cause that London Bridge concentrated upon itself so much of the life of the nation, and that the town which that bridge served, always the largest commercial city, became at last the capital of the island.

We have already said that the establishment of the site of London Bridge was a capital point in the history of the river and the principal line of division in its course. What were the topographical conditions which caused the river to be crossed at this point rather than at another?

It is always of the greatest moment to men to find some crossing for a great river as low down as may be towards the mouth. For the higher the bridge the longer the detour between, at the least, two provinces of the country which the river traverses. It is especially important to find such a crossing as low down as possible when the river is tidal and when it is flanked upon either side by great flooded marshes, as was and is the Thames. For under such conditions it is difficult, especially in primitive times, to cross habitually from one side to the other in boats.

Now it is a universal rule of early topography, and one which can be proved upon twenty of the old trackways of England, that the wild path which the earliest men used, when it approaches a river, seeks out a spur of higher and drier land, and if possible one directly facing another similar spur upon the far side of the water. It is a feature which the present writer continually observed in the exploration of the old British trackway between Winchester and Canterbury; it is similarly observable in the presumably British track between Chester and Manchester; and it is the feature which determined the site of London Bridge.

From the sea for sixty miles is a succession of what was once entirely, and is now still in great part, marshy land; or at least if

55

there are no marshes upon one bank there will be marshes upon the other. In the rare places down stream where there is a fairly rapid rise upon either side of the river the stream is far too wide for bridging; and these marshes were to be found right up the valley until one struck the gravel at Chelsea: even here there were bad marshes on the farther shore.

There is in the whole or the upper stretch of the tidal water but one place where a bluff of high and dry land faces, not indeed land equally dry immediately upon the farther bank, but at least a spur of dry land which approaches fairly near to the main stream. If the modern contour lines be taken and laid out upon a map of London this spur will be found to project from Southwark northward directly towards the river, and immediately opposite it is the dry hill, surrounded upon three sides by river or by marsh, upon which grew up the settlement of London. Here, then, the first crossing of the Thames was certain to be made.

It is not known whether a permanent bridge existed before the Roman Conquest. It may be urged in favour of the negative argument that Cæsar had no knowledge of such a bridge, or at least did not march towards it, but crossed the river with difficulty in the higher reaches by a ford. And it may also be urged that a bridge across the Rhine was equally unknown in that time. But, the bridge once established, it could not fail to become the main point of convergence for the commerce of Southern England, and indeed for much of that which proceeded from the North upon its way to the Continent. Such an obstacle would oppose itself to every invasion, and did, in fact, oppose itself to more than one historical invasion from the North Sea. It would further prevent sea-going vessels whose masts were securely stepped and could not lower from proceeding farther up stream, and would thereupon become the boundary of the seaport of the Thames. Such a bridge would, again, concentrate upon itself the traffic of all that important and formerly wealthy part of the island which bulges out to the east between the estuary of the Thames and the Wash, and which must necessarily have desired communication both with the still wealthier southern portion and with the Continent. But, more important than this, London Bridge also concentrated upon itself all the up-country traffic in men and in goods which came in by the natural gate of the country at the Straits of Dover, except that small portion which happened to be proceeding to the south-west of England: and this exception to the early commerce of England was the smaller from the comparative ease with which the Channel could be crossed between Brittany and Cornwall.

Finally, the Bridge, as it formed the limit for sea-going vessels, formed also if not the limit at least a convenient terminus for craft coming from inland down the stream. It would form the place of transhipment between the sea-going and the inland trade.

Everything then conspired to make this first crossing of the Thames the chief commercial point in Britain; and, since we are considering in particular the history of the river, it must be noted that these conditions also made of London Bridge what we have remarked it to be, the chief division in the whole course of the stream. This character it still maintains, and the life of the river from the bridge to the Nore is a totally different thing, with a different literature and a different accompanying art, from the life of the river above bridges.

We have seen that the river when it is regarded as an avenue of access to men for commerce or for travel is, especially in early times, and with boats of light draught, of one piece from Lechlade to London Bridge. There was in this section always sufficient water even in a dry summer to float some sort of a boat. But the river, regarded as a barrier or obstacle for human beings in their movement up and down Britain, did not form one such united section. On the contrary, it divided itself, as all such rivers do, into two very clearly defined parts: there was that upper part which could be crossed at frequent intervals by an army, that lower part in which fords are rare.

In most rivers one has nothing more to do in describing those two sections than to show how gradually they merge into one another. In most rivers the passage of the upper waters is perfectly easy, and as one descends the fords get rarer and rarer, until at last they cease.

With the Thames this is not the case. The two portions of the river are sharply divided in the vicinity of Oxford, and that for reasons which we have already seen when we were speaking of the suitability of its banks for habitation. The upper Thames is indeed shallow and narrow, and there are innumerable places above Oxford where it could be crossed, so far as the volume of its waters was concerned. It was crossed by husbandmen wherever a village or a farm stood upon its banks. Perhaps the highest point at which it had to be crossed at one chosen spot is to be discovered in the word Somer_ford_ Keynes, but the ease with which the water itself could be traversed is apparent rather in the absence than in the presence of names of this sort upon the upper Thames. Shifford, for instance, which used to be spelt Siford, may just as well have been named from the crossing of the Great Brook as from the crossing of the Thames. The only other is Duxford.

While, however, the upper Thames was thus easy to cross

57

where individuals only or small groups of cattle were concerned, the marshes on either side always made it difficult for an army. The records of early fighting are meagre, and often legendary, but such as they are you do not find the upper Thames crossed and recrossed as are the upper Severn or the upper Trent. There are two points of passage: Cricklade and Oxford, nor can the passage from Oxford be made westward over the marshes. It is confined to the ford going north and south.

Below Oxford, after the entry of the Cherwell, and from thence down to a point not very easily determined, but which is perhaps best fixed at Wallingford, the Thames is only passable at fixed crossings in ordinary weather, as at Sandford, where the hard gravels approach the bank upon either side, and at other places, each distant from the next by long stretches of river.

It is not easy, now that the river has been locked, to determine precisely where all these original crossings are to be found.

The records of Abingdon and its bridge make it certain that a difficult ford existed here; the name "Burford" attached to the bridge points to the ancient ford at this spot. It is a name to be discovered in several other parts of England where there has been some ancient crossing of a river, as, for instance, the crossing of the Mole in Surrey by the Roman military road.

The next place below Abingdon may have been at Appleford, but was more likely between the high cliff at Clifton-Hampden and the high and dry spit of Long Wittenham. Below this again for miles there was no easy crossing of the river.

The Thames was certainly impassable at Dorchester. The whole importance of Dorchester indeed in history lies in its being a strong fortified position, and it depends for its defence upon the depth of the river, which swirls round the peninsula occupied by the camp.

It has been conjectured that there was a Roman ford or ferry at the east end of Little Wittenham Wood, where it touches the river. The conjecture is ill supported. No track leads to this spot from the south, and close by is an undoubted ford where now stands Shillingford Bridge.

Below this again there was no crossing until one got to Wallingford; and here we reach a point of the greatest importance in the history of the Thames and of England.

Wallingford was not the lowest point at which the Thames could ever be crossed. So far was this from being the case that the tidal Thames could be crossed in several places on the ebb, notably at the passage between Ealing and Kew, where Kew Bridge now stands; and, as we shall see, the Thames was passable at many other places. But the special character of the passage at Wallingford lay in the fact that it was a ford upon which one could always depend. Below Wallingford the crossings were either only to be effected in very dry seasons or, though normally usable, might be interrupted by rain.

It is at Wallingford, therefore, that the main lowest passage of the Thames was effected, and it was through Wallingford that Berkshire communicated with the Chilterns. Wallingford is, then, the second point of division upon the Thames when one is regarding that river as a defence or a boundary. Below Wallingford there was perhaps a regular crossing at Pangbourne; there was certainly a ford of great importance between Streatley and Goring; and all the way down the river at intervals were difficult but practicable passages— notably at Cowey Stakes between the Surrey and the Middlesex shore, a place which is the traditional crossing of Cæsar. The water here in normal weather was, however, as much as five feet deep, and this ford well illustrates the difficulties of all the lower crossings of the Thames.

The effect of the river as a barrier must, of course, have largely depended upon the level to which the waters rose in early times. It is exceedingly difficult to get any evidence upon this—first, because however far you go back in English history some sort of control seems always to have been imposed upon the river; and secondly, because the early overflows have left little permanent effect.

As an example of the antiquity of the regulation of the Thames we have the embankment round the Isle of Dogs, which is Roman or pre-Roman in its origin, like the sea-wall of the Wash, which defends the Fenland; and at Ealing, Staines, Abingdon, and twenty other places we have sites probably pre-historic, and certainly at the beginnings of history, which could never have been inhabited if the neighbouring fields had not been drained or protected. The regularity of the stream has therefore been somewhat artificial throughout all the centuries of recorded history, and the banks have had ample time to acquire consistency.

It is certain, of course, that works of planting, of draining, or of embankment, which required continuous energy, skill, and capital, decayed after the coming of the Saxon pirates, and were not undertaken again with full vigour until after the Norman Conquest. Even to-day the work is not quite complete, though every year sees its improvement: we are still unable to prevent regularly recurrent floods in the flats round Oxford and below the gorge of the Chilterns; but for the purpose of this argument the chief fact to be noted is that no serious interruption to the approach of the river seems to have existed in historic times.

In pre-historic times many stretches of the river must have afforded great difficulties of approach. The mouths of the Ock, the Coln, the Kennet, the Mole, and the Wandle must each have been surrounded by a marsh; all the plain between Oxford and the Hinkseys must have been partially flooded, as must the upper reaches between Lechlade and Witham (on one side or the other of the stream as it winds from the southern to the northern rises of land), and as must also have been the long stretch of the right bank below Reading. The highest spring tides may have been felt as high up the stream as Staines, and both the character of the surface and the contour lines permit one to conjecture that the valley of the Wandle and several other inlets from the lower river were flooded. Yet it is remarkable that in this alluvium, more disturbed and dug than any other in Europe, little or nothing of human relics, of boats, or of piles has been discovered, and this absence of testimony also points to the remoteness of date from which we should reckon the human control of the river.

Here, as in many other conjectures concerning early history or pre-history, one is convinced of that safe rule which, in Europe at least, bids us never exaggerate the changes achieved by the last few centuries or the contrast between recorded and unrecorded things.

The tendency of most modern history in this country has been to exaggerate such changes and such contrasts. In the greater part of modern popular history care is taken to emphasise the difference between the Middle and Dark Ages and the last few centuries. The forests of England are represented as impassable, or nearly so; the numbers of the population are grossly underestimated; the towns which have had a continuous municipal existence of 1500 years are represented as villages.

The same spirit would tend to make of the Thames Valley in the Dark and Middle Ages a very different landscape from that which we see to-day. The floods were indeed more common and the passage of the river somewhat more difficult; cultivation did not everywhere approach the banks as it does now; and in two or three spots where there has been a great development of modern building, notably at Reading, and, of course, in London, the banks have been artificially strengthened. But with these exceptions it may be confidently asserted that no belt of densely inhabited landscape in England has changed so little in its natural features as the Thames Valley.

There are dozens of reaches upon the upper Thames where little is in sight save the willows, the meadows, and a village church tower, which present exactly the same aspect to-day as they did when that church was first built. You might put a man of the fifteenth century on to the water below St. John's Lock, and, until he came to Buscot Lock, he would hardly know that he had passed into a time other than his own. The same steeple of Lechlade would stand as a permanent landmark beyond the fields, and, a long way off, the same church of Eaton Hastings, which he had known, would show above the trees.

There is another method of judging the comparative smallness of the change, and it is a method which can be applied to many other parts of England whose desertion or wildness in the Dark and early Middle Ages has been too confidently asserted. That method is to note where human settlements were and are found. With the exception of the long and probably marshy piece between Radcot and Shifford the whole of the upper Thames was dotted with such settlements, which, though small, were quite close to the banks. Kelmscott is right up against the river in what one would otherwise have imagined to be land too marshy for building until modern times. Buscot, on the other bank, is not only close to the river, but was a royal manor of high historical importance in the eleventh century. Eaton Hastings is similarly placed right against the bank; so was in its day the palace of Kempsford above Lechlade, and so is the church of Inglesham between the two. All the way down you have at intervals old stonework and old place names, indicating habitation upon the upper Thames.

A proper system of locks is comparatively modern on any European river. The invention is even said (upon doubtful authority) to be as late as the sixteenth century, but the method of regulating the waters of a river by weirs is immemorial.

We have no earlier record of weirs upon the Thames than that in Magna Charta; but some such system must have existed from the time when men first used the Thames in a regular manner for commerce.

There is but one place left in which one can still reconstruct for oneself the aspect of such weirs as were till but little more than a century ago the universal method of canalising the river. Modern weirs are merely adjuncts to locks, and are usually found upon a branch of the stream other than that which leads up to the lock. But in this weir the old fashion of crossing the whole stream is still preserved. There is no lock, and when a boat would pass up or down the paddles of the weir have to be lifted. It is, in a modern journey upon the upper Thames, the one faint incident which the day affords, for if one is going down the stream but few paddles are lifted, and the boat shoots a small rapid, while to admit a boat going up stream the whole weir is raised, and, even so, a great rush of water opposes the boat as it is hauled through. Some years ago there were several of these weirs upon the upper river. They have all been superseded by locks, and it is probable that this last one will not long survive.

Such weirs did certainly sufficiently regulate the stream as to make its banks regularly habitable. If no local order, at least the interest of villagers in their mills sufficed to the watching of the stream.

We have in the place names upon the Thames a further evidence of the antiquity of its regulation, for, as will be seen in a moment, none give proof of any important settlement later than the eleventh century.

These place names not only indicate a continuous and early settlement of the banks, but also form in themselves a very interesting series, whose etymology is a little section of the history of England.

Of purely Celtic names very few survive in the sites of human habitation, though the names of the waterways are almost universally Celtic, as is the name of Thames itself. But it is probable that in the Saxon names which line the river there are many corruptions of Celtic words made to sound in the Saxon fashion. We cannot prove such origins. We can surmise with justice that the "tons" and "dons" all up and down England are Celtic terminations; they are almost unknown in Germany. There is a somewhat pedantic guess, drawn (it is said) from Iceland, that we got this national name ending from Scandinavia; so universal a habit would hardly have arisen from an admixture of Scandinavian blood received at the very close of the Dark Ages and affecting but small patches of North England. Moreover, as against this theory, there is the fact that quite half the Celtic place names mentioned in our early history and in that of Gaul had a similar termination. London itself is the best example.

If, however, we neglect this termination, and consider the first part of the words in which it occurs (as in Abing-don, Bensing-ton, Ea-ton, etc.), we shall find that most of the place names are Saxon in form, and some certainly Saxon in derivation.

Thus Ea-ton, a name scattered all along the Thames, from its very source to the last reaches, is the "tun" by the water or stream. Clif-ton (as in Clifton-Hampden) is the "ton" on the cliff, a very marked feature of the left bank of the river at this place. Of Bensing-ton, now Benson, we know nothing, nor do we of the origin of the word Abing-don.

The names terminating in "ham" are, in their termination at least, certainly Teutonic; and the same may be true of most of those—but not all of those—ending in "ford." Ford may just as well

62

be a Celtic as a Teutonic ending, and in either case means a "passage," a "going." It does not even in all cases indicate a shallow passage, though in the great majority of cases on the Thames it does indicate a place where one could cross the river on foot. Thus Wallingford was probably the walled or embattled ford, and Oxford almost certainly the "ford of the droves"—droves going north from Berkshire. One may say roughly that all the "hams" were Teutonic save where one can put one's finger on a probable Celtic derivation such as one has, for instance, in the case of Witham, which should mean the settlement upon the "bend" or curve of the river, a Celtic name with a Teutonic ending.

One may also believe that the termination "or" or "ore" is Teutonic; Cumnor may have meant "the wayfarers' stage," and Windsor probably "the landing place on the winding of the river."

Hythe also is thought to be Teutonic. One can never be quite sure with a purely Anglo-Saxon word, that it had a German origin, but at least Hythe is Anglo-Saxon, a wharf or stage; thus Bablock Hythe on the road through the Roman town of Eynsham across the river to Cumnor and Abingdon, cutting off the great bend of the river at Witham; so also the town we now call "Maidenhead," which was perhaps the "mid-Hythe" between Windsor and Reading. Some few certainly Celtic names do survive: in the Sinodun Hills, for instance, above Dorchester; and the first part of the name Dorchester itself is Celtic. At the very head of the Thames you have Coates, reminding one of the Celtic name for the great wood that lay along the hill; but just below, where the water begins, to flow, Kemble and Ewen, if they are Saxon, are perhaps drawn from the presence of a "spring." Cricklade may be all Celtic, or may be partly Celtic and partly Saxon. London is Celtic, as we have seen. And in the mass of places whose derivation it is impossible to establish the primitive roots of a Celtic place name may very possibly survive.

The purely Roman names have quite disappeared, and, what is odd, they disappeared more thoroughly in the Thames Valley than in any other part of England. Dorchester alone preserves a faint reminiscence of its Romano-Celtic name; but Bicester to the north, and the crossing of the ways at Alchester, are probably Saxon in the first part at least. Streatley has a Roman derivation, as have so many similar names throughout England which stand upon a "strata" or "way" of British or of Roman origin. But though "Spina" is still Speen, Ad Pontes, close by, one of the most important points upon the Roman Thames, has lost its Roman name entirely, and is known as Staines: the stones or stone which marked the head of the jurisdiction of London upon the river.

To return to the river regarded as a boundary, it is subject to this rather interesting historical observation that it has been more of a boundary in highly civilised than in barbaric times.

One would expect the exact contrary to be the case. A civilised man can cross a river more easily than a barbarian; and in civilised times there are permanent bridges, where in barbaric times there would be only fords or ferries.

Nevertheless, it is true of the Thames, as of nearly every other division in Europe, that it was much more of a boundary at the end of the Roman Empire, and is more of a strict boundary to-day, than it was during the Dark Ages, and presumably also before the Claudian invasion. Thus we may conjecture with a fair accuracy that in the last great ordering of boundaries within the Roman Empire, which was the work of Diocletian, and so much of which still survives in our European politics to-day (for instance, the boundary of Normandy), the Thames formed the division between Southern and Midland Britain. It is equally certain that it did not form any exact division between Wessex and Mercia.

The estuary has, of course, always formed a division, and in the barbarian period it separated the higher civilisation of Kent from that of the East Saxons, who were possibly of a different race, and certainly of a different culture. But the Thames above London Bridge was not a true boundary until the civilisation of England began to form, towards the close of the Dark Ages. It is perpetually crossed and recrossed by contending armies, and the first result of a success is to cause the conqueror to annex a belt from the farther bank to his own territories.

It is further remarkable that the one great definite boundary of the Dark Ages in England—that which was established for a few years by Alfred between his kingdom and the territory of the Danish invaders—abandons the Thames above bridges altogether, and uses it as a limitation in its estuarial part only, up to the mouth of the Lea.

With the definition of exact frontiers for the English counties, however, a process whose origin can hardly antedate the Norman Conquest by many years, the Thames at once becomes of the utmost importance as a boundary.

Its higher and hardly navigable streams are not so used. The upper Thames and its little tributaries for some ten miles from its source are not only indifferent to county boundaries, but run through a territory which has been singularly indefinite in the past. For instance, the parish of Kemble, wherein the first waters now appear, has been counted now in Gloucester, now in Wilts. But when these ten miles are run, just after Castle Eaton Bridge, and not quite half way between that bridge and the old royal palace at

Kempsford, the Thames becomes the line of division between two counties, and from there to the sea it never loses its character of a boundary.

It is a tribute to the great place of the river in history that there is no other watercourse in England nor any other natural division of which this is so universally true.

The reason that the Thames, like so many other European boundaries, has come late into the process of demarcation, and the reason that its use as a limit is more apparent in civilised than in uncivilised times, is simply the fact that limits and boundaries themselves are never of great exactitude save in times of comparatively high civilisation. It is when a complex system of law and a far-reaching power of execution are present in a country that the necessity for precise delimitation arises. In the barbaric period of England there was no such necessity. Doubtless the men of Berkshire and the men of Oxfordshire felt themselves to be in general divided by the stream; but had we documents to hand (which, of course, we have not) it might be possible to show that exceptional tracts, such as the isolated Hill of Witham (which is much more influenced by Oxford than by Abingdon), was treated as the land of Oxfordshire men in early times, or was perhaps a territory in dispute; and something of the same sort may have existed in the connection of Caversham with Reading.

In this old age of our civilisation the exactitude of the boundary which the Thames establishes is apparent in various survivals. Islands now joined to the one bank and indistinguishable from the rest of the shore are still annexed to the farther shore. Such a patch is to be found at Streatley, geographically in Berkshire, legally in Oxford; there is another opposite Staines, which Middlesex claims from Surrey. In all, half-a-dozen or more such anomalous frontiers mark the course of the old river. One arrested in process of formation may be seen at Pentonhook.

A boundary—that is, an obstacle to travel—has this further feature, that the point at which it is crossed—that is, the point at which the obstacle is surmounted—is certain to become a point of strategic and often of commercial importance. So it is with the passes over mountains and with the narrows of the sea, and so it is with fords and bridges over rivers. So it is with the Thames.

The energies both of travel and of war are driven towards and confined in such spots. Fortresses arise and towns which they may defend. Depots of goods are formed, the coining and the change of money are established, secure meeting places for speculation are founded.

Such passages over the Thames were of two sorts: there are

65

first the original fords, numerous and primeval; next the crossing places of the great roads.

Of the original fords we have already drawn up a list. Few have, merely as fords, proved to be of strategic or commercial value. Oxford may have been an early exception; and the difficult passage at Abingdon founded a great monastery but no military post: the rise of each was connected, as was Reading (which had no ford), with the junction of a tributary. Wallingford alone, in its character of the last easy and practicable ford down the river, had for centuries an importance certainly due to geographical causes alone. Two principal events of English history—the crossing of the Thames by the Conqueror and the successful challenge of Henry II. to Stephen—depend upon the site of this crossing. Long before their time it had been of capital importance to the Saxon kings, so early as Offa and so late as Alfred. If the bridges built at Abingdon in the fifteenth century had not gradually deflected the western road, Wallingford might still count the fourteen churches and the large population which it possessed for so many centuries.

Apart from Wallingford, however, the fords, as fords, did little to build up towns or to determine the topography of English history. Of more importance were the crossings of the great roads.

When one remembers that the south of England was originally by far the wealthiest part of the country, and when one considers the shape of Ireland, it is evident that certain main tracks would lead from north to south, and that most or all of these would be compelled to cross the Thames Valley. We find four such primeval ways.

One from the Straits of Dover in the south-east to the north-western centres of the Welsh Marches and of Chester, the Port for Ireland, and so up west of the Pennines. This came in Saxon times to be called the Watling Street, a name common to other lesser lanes.

Another, the converse to this, proceeded from the metal mines of the south-west to the north-east until it struck and merged into other roads running north and east of the Pennines. This came to be called (as did other lesser roads) the Fosse Way.

A third went more sharply west from the southern districts, and connected them not with the Dee, but with the lower Severn. This track ran from the open highlands of Hampshire through Newbury and the Berkshire Hills to Gloucester, and was called (like other lesser tracks) the Ermine Street.

Finally, a fourth went in a great bend from these same highlands up eastward to the coast of the North Sea in East Anglia. This was called in Saxon times the Icknield Way.

66

All these can be traced in their general direction throughout and for most of their length minutely. All were forced to cross the Thames Valley, which so nearly divided the whole of South England from east to west.

Of these four crossings the first in point of interest is that which the Ermine Street makes over the upper Thames at Cricklade.

These old roads are of capital importance in the story of England, and though historians have always recognised this there are a number of features about them which have not been sufficiently noted—as, for instance, that armies until perhaps the twelfth century perpetually used them; for the great English roads, though their general track was laid out in pre-historic times, were generally hardened, straightened, and embanked by the Romans in a manner which permitted them to survive right on into the early Middle Ages; and of these four all were so hardened and strengthened, except the Icknield Way. Not one of them is quite complete to-day, but the Ermine Street is perhaps the best preserved. It is a good modern road all the way from Bayden to Gloucester, with the exception of a very slight gap at this village of Cricklade.

It originally crossed the river half-a-mile below Cricklade Bridge, so that the priory which stood on the left bank lay just to the south of the old road. How and when the old bridge at Cricklade fell we have no record, but one of the most important records of the Thames in Anglo-Saxon history is connected with this passage of the river.

The importance of Cricklade as a station upon the upper Thames does not only proceed from its being the crossing place of a great road, it is also the point when the first important tributary stream, the Churn, joins the Thames. Above this junction the Thames nowadays is hardly a stream; and even in the eighteenth century and earlier, before the digging of the Severn and Thames Canal, it must have depended on the weather whether there were any appreciable amount of water in the upper part or not. It would probably be found, if records could be examined, that the mills at Somerford Keynes were not continually worked throughout the year, even when the supply of water had been left undiminished by modern engineering. But when once the Churn (which, as we have seen, has a larger volume of water than the Thames) had fallen in at Cricklade the two formed a true river, with depth in it always sufficient to support a boat, and with a fairly strong stream, as also with a width sufficient for minor traffic; and it is after Cricklade that you get a succession of villages and churches dependent upon the river and standing close to its banks.

But though this piece of hydrography has its importance the chief meaning of Cricklade in history lay in the fact that it was the spot where this Ermine Street on its way from the south country to the Severn Valley got over the Thames, and the village connected with it was entrenched certainly in Roman and probably in pre-Roman times. This entrenchment may still be traced.

The crossing of the Thames by the Icknield Way, unlike the crossing of the Ermine Street at Cricklade, presents a problem.

Cricklade, as we have seen, is a perfectly well-established site, and we owe our certitude upon the matter to the fact that the Romans had hardened and straightened what was probably an old British track. But with the crossing of the Icknield Way no such complete certitude exists, for the Icknield Way was but a vague barbarian track, often tortuous in outline, confused by branching ways, and presenting all the features of a savage trail. Doubtless that trail was used during the four hundred years of the high Roman civilisation as a country road, just as the similar trail, known as the "Pilgrims' Way" from Winchester to Canterbury, was used in the same epoch. There are plenty of Roman remains to be found along the track, and there is no doubt that all such roads, even when the State was not at the expense of hardening or straightening them, were in continual use before, as they were in continual use after, the presence of Roman government in this island; but the Icknield Way does not approach the river in a clear and unmistakable manner as would a Roman or a Romanised road. It is on this account that the exact point of its crossing has been debated.

The problem is roughly this: the high and treeless chalk downs have been used from the beginning of human habitation in these islands as the principal highways, and any single traveller or tribe that desired in early times to get from the Hampshire highlands to the east and north of England must have begun by following the ridge of the Berkshire Hills, and by continuing along the dry upland of the Chiltern Hills, which continue this reach beyond the Thames. But the spot at which the pre-historic crossing of the Thames was effected cannot be determined by a simple survey of the place where the Thames cuts through the chalk range. Wallingford up above this gorge has certain claims, both because it was the lowest of the continually practicable fords upon the river, and because its whole history points to an immemorial antiquity. Higher still, Dorchester, on which every historian of the Thames must dwell as perhaps the most interesting of all the settlements upon the banks of the river, has also been suggested. Just above Dorchester, on the Berkshire side, stands the peculiar isolated twin height which forms so conspicuous a landmark when one gazes over the plain from the summit of the Downs. Such landmarks often helped to trace the old roads. And Dorchester has also an immemorial antiquity—a pre-historic fortification upon the hills above, and fortifications, probably historic, on the Oxford bank below, but Dorchester has no ford.

When all the evidence is weighed it seems more probable that the regular crossing from the Berkshire Hills to the Chilterns was effected at Streatley.

Of this there are several proofs. In the first place, the name of the place suggests the passage of some great way. Place names of this sort are invariably found upon some one of the principal roads of England. In the second place, a lane bearing the traditional name of the Icknield Way can be traced to a point very near the river and the village. Another can be recovered beyond the river. The name would hardly have been so continued—even with considerable gaps—both upon the Oxfordshire and the Berkshire side unless the place of regular crossing had been here.

Within a mile or two of Streatley this lane begins to descend the side of the Berkshire Downs. Just before it falls into the Wantage Road and is lost it has begun to curl round the shoulder of the steep hill; but there is no way of telling at what precise spot it would strike the river upon the Berkshire side, because a thousand years or so of building, cultivation, and other changes have obliterated every trace of it.

Luckily, we have some indication upon the farther bank. A way can then be traced here as a lane (and in the gaps as a right of way, as a path, or sometimes only by its general direction) for some miles on the Oxfordshire side as it approaches Goring and the river coming from the Chilterns. And we know the point at which it strikes the village. This point is at the Sloane Hotel close to the railway; the inn is actually built upon the old road. Beyond the railway the track is continued in the lane which leads on past the schoolhouse to the old ferry, where there was presumably in Roman times a ford. If we accept this track we can conjecture that the vicarage of Streatley, upon the Berkshire bank, stands upon the continuation of the Way, and give the place where the pre-historic road crossed the river with tolerable certitude, though it is, I believe, impossible to recover the half-mile or so which lies between Streatley vicarage and the point where the Wantage Road and the Icknield Way separated upon the hillside above.

If the ford lay here the site was certainly well chosen, just below a group of islands which broadened the stream and made it at once shallower and less swift, acting somewhat as a natural weir above the crossing.

The third crossing place of a great pre-historic road, that of the Watling Street, is believed to correspond with the line of that very ugly suspension bridge which runs from Lambeth to the Horseferry Road in Westminster. This is, according to the most probable conjecture, the place at which the great road which ran from the Straits of Dover to the north-western ports of the island crossed the Thames.

Here, of course, there could be no question of a ford; there can only have been a ferry. Such a ferry existed throughout the Middle Ages and up to the building of Westminster Bridge, and produced a large revenue for the Archbishop of Canterbury. The memory of it is preserved in the name of the street upon the Middlesex shore. The Watling Street is fairly fixed in all its journey from the coast to the Archbishop's palace on the banks of the river. On the Middlesex shore it is lost, but it may be conjectured to have run in a curve somewhere in the neighbourhood of Buckingham Palace up on the higher ground west of the Tybourne, parallel with or perhaps identical with Park Lane until we find it certainly again at the Marble Arch, whence in the form of the Edgware Road it begins a clear track across North-Western England.

As for the Fosse Way, it only just touches the valley of the Thames. It crosses the line of the river in a high embankment a mile or so below its traditional source at Thames head, but above the point where the first water is seen. A small culvert running under that embankment takes the flood water in winter down the hollow, but no longer covers a regular stream.

Besides these four crossings of the old British ways above London Bridge there is the crossing of the Roman Road at Staines, which may or may not represent a passage older than the Roman occupation. We have no proof of its being older. The river is deep, and, unless the broken causeway on the Surrey shore is regarded as the remains of British work, there is no trace of a pre-Roman track in the neighbourhood.

The crossing at Staines was the main bridge over the middle river during the Roman occupation; no other spot on the banks (except London Bridge) is certainly the site of a Roman bridge.

But apart from these there are two unsolved problems in connection with the roads across the Thames Valley in Roman times. The first concerns the passage of the upper Thames south of Eynsham; the second concerns the road which runs south from Bicester and Alchester.

As to the first of these, we know that the plain lying to the north of the Thames between the Cotswolds and the Chilterns was thoroughly occupied. We have also in the Saxon Chronicle a

70

legendary account of the occupation of four Roman towns in this plain by the Saxon invaders. By what avenue did this wealthy and civilised district communicate with the wealthy and civilised south?

It is a question which will probably never be answered. There is no trace remaining of Roman bridges; perhaps nothing was built save of wood.

The obvious short-cut from the Roman town of Eynsham across the Witham peninsula to Abingdon bears no signs of a ford approached by Roman work or of a bridge, nor any record of such things.

As to the second question, the road from Bicester southward runs straight to Dorchester. At Dorchester, as we have seen, there was no ford, though just below it a Roman ferry has been guessed at.

There may have been a country road running down along the left or north bank of the river to the pre-historic crossing place at Goring and Streatley; but if there was, no trace of it remains, save perhaps in the two place names North Stoke and South Stoke.

A barrier has yet another quality in history, and that quality is perhaps the most important of all. In so far as it is an obstacle it is also a means of defence.

All the great rivers of Europe prove this. They are studded with lines of strongholds standing either right upon their banks or close by; and various as is the character of the different great rivers in their physical conformation, few or none have been unable to furnish sites for fortification. For instance, the slow rivers of Northern France, running for the most part through a flat country, were able to afford fortresses for the Gaulish clans in their numerous islands; the origin of Melun and Paris, for instance, was of this kind. The sharp rocks along the Rhone became platforms for castle after castle: Beaucaire, Tarascon, Aries, Avignon, and twenty others all of this sort.

The Thames, curiously enough, forms an exception; it is an exception even in the list of English rivers, most of which can show a certain number of fortifications along their banks.

In the whole course of the great river above London there are but three examples of fortification, or at any rate of fortification directly dependent upon the river. Of these the first, at Lechlade, is conjectural; the second, at Windsor, came quite late in history, and the only one which seems to have been a primeval fortified site was Dorchester.

There were, of course, plenty of towns and castles susceptible of defence. At one time or another every important settlement upon the Thames was capable of resistance: Oxford was walled,

Wallingford was a fortress, Abingdon or Reading could be defended. But these were all, so to speak, artificial. The settlement came first, and after the settlement the necessity of guarding it from attack, and it was so guarded, not by natural means, but by human construction. The castle at Oxford, for instance, stood upon a mound of earth raised by human work. The only considerable place in which the river itself suggested defence from the earliest times appears to have been at Dorchester.

The curious importance of Dorchester in the very origins of English history and the still more curious way in which it sinks out of sight for generations, to revive again in the tenth century, is one of the puzzles of the history of the Thames.

It is useless to pursue an archæological discussion as to the origin of the place, and still more useless to try and determine why, though certainly the most easily defended, it should originally have been the only heavily fortified spot in the whole of the valley. We know that it was Roman: we know that it was a place of pre-historic fortification before the Romans came: we know that a Roman road ran northward towards Bicester from it, and we also know, or at least we can make a very probable guess, that though it was continuously important, and that the interest of early history is continually returning to it, it can never have been large.

Perhaps the best conjecture upon the origin of Dorchester is that the stronghold grew up as an out-lier to the great fort over the river at the top of Sinodun Hill. The exact and regular peninsula between the bend in the Thames and the mouth of the Thames is obviously suited for fortification: the tributary flows just to the east of this peninsula, exactly parallel with the main river beyond, and covers the peninsula not only with a stream on its east flank, but with a marsh at the mouth. One can imagine that the conspicuous heights of the Sinodun Hills were held, from the very beginning of human habitation in this district, as a permanent fortress, into which the neighbouring tribes could retire during war, and one can imagine that when the river was low in summer, and perhaps fordable, the spit of land before it, which formed an exception to the marshes round about, needed to be protected as a sort of bastion beyond the stream. This theory will at least account for the two great ridges of earthwork going from one water to the other and completely cutting off the peninsula, since it is agreed these works are earlier than the Roman invasion. Whatever its origin, the part which Dorchester plays in the early history of England is most remarkable.

The conversion of England was effected by a process of which we know far more than of any other series of national events before the Danish invasions. That process is more exactly recorded, less legendary, and more consecutively told because it was (to all contemporary watchers) the capital event of the time, and to all posterity the one thing that explained men to themselves.

We know also that, not so much the nucleus of the conversion as the secure vantage from which it marched outward, was the triangle of Kent. We can believe that the civilisation of Kent was something quite separate from the rest of the south-eastern portion of England, and that the many customary survivals which are, to this day, native to the county are remaining proofs of its unique character among the petty kingdoms during the mythical period between the withdrawal of the Romans and the arrival of St. Augustine.

The early hold of civilisation upon Kent is explicable. But when the influence of Rome begins to spread again over England you have distances covered which are astounding; there occur sporadic incidents of the highest importance in spots where they would be the least expected. Among the very first of these is the first baptism of a West-Saxon King.

It was certainly at Dorchester that this baptism took place and the choice of the site, little as we know of the village or city, has filled every historian with conjecture. Up to the very landing of St. Augustine we are still dependent upon what is half legendary and very meagre record. The chief point indeed as regards this part of the country is the tradition of a battle fought against the British at Bedford by the West Saxons and the occupation of "four towns." This success was put down by tradition to the year 571, but everything was still so dark that even this success is a legend.

Within the lifetime of a man you have the baptism of Cynegil, the king of the West Saxons, at Dorchester, and that baptism takes place less than forty years after the complete submission of Kent.

The Chronicle, in mentioning this date, is no longer upon legendary ground: it is dealing with an event which was kept on record by civilised men who understood the art of writing, who could speak Latin, who could bear their records to Rome, and, what is more, the fact and the date are confirmed by the Venerable Bede.

It is imagined by some authorities that the fulness of the story and its apparent accuracy depend upon access to some early ecclesiastical record preserved at Dorchester and now lost. At any rate, Dorchester, whether because it had been, up till then, an unconquered Roman town, or for whatever other reason, becomes at once the ecclesiastical centre and one to which, even when this baptism takes place, the King of Northumbria was at the pains of travelling southward to, to be present as sponsor for the new Christian.

The story has a special historical interest, because it shows how very vague were the boundaries and the occupancies of the little wandering chieftains of this period. It need hardly be pointed out that no regular division into shires can have existed so early, and, as we have already insisted, the Thames itself was not a permanent boundary between any two definable societies, yet those who regard the Anglo-Saxon Chronicle as historical would show one Penda had appeared a few years before as the chief of a group of men with a new name, the Mercians—probably a loose agglomeration of tribes occupying the middle strip of England; a group whose dialect and measures of land are, perhaps, the ancestors of the modern Midland dialect and most of our measures. Cynegil's baptism could not have taken place in territory controlled by Penda, for he was the champion of all the Anti-Christian forces of the time, and though he had just defeated the West Saxons, and (according to a later legend) pushed back their boundary to the line of the Thames, his action, like that of all the little kings of the barbaric age in Britain, can have been no more than a march with a few thousands, a battle, and a retreat. In a word, the true and verifiable story of Cynegil's baptism is one of the many valuable instances which help to prove the unreliability of that part of the early Chronicle which does not deal with ecclesiastical affairs.

The priest who received Cynegil into the Church was one Birinus, an Italian, and perhaps a Milanese; he appears, from his first presence in Dorchester, to have fixed the seat of a bishopric in that village. His reasons for choosing the spot are as impossible to discover as are the origins of any other of the characteristics of the place. It was, in any case, as were so many of the sees of the Dark Ages, a frontier see—a sort of ecclesiastical fortress, pushed out to the very limits of the occupation of the enemy.

Whether Dorchester continued to be a bishopric from this moment onwards we cannot tell; but no less than three hundred years afterwards—in the tenth century—it appears again, and this time as the centre of the gigantic diocese which stretched throughout the whole of Middle England and right up to the Humber. The Conquest came, the diocese was cut up just afterwards, and the seat of the bishop finally removed from the village to Lincoln, and with the Conquest the importance of Dorchester as a fortified position, an importance which it had held for untold centuries, began to decline in favour of Oxford.

The artificial chain of fortifications up the Thames Valley, which had their origin under William the Conqueror, will call our attention to many other spots besides Oxford as these pages proceed, but it is interesting at this moment to consider Oxford in its early military aspect, when it succeeded Dorchester, and came forward as the chief stronghold of the upper Thames Valley above Wallingford.

The gravel bank north of the ford, by which what is presumed to have been the drovers' road from south to north crossed the river, had supported a very considerable population, and had attained a very considerable civil importance, long before the Conquest. It is difficult to believe that any new, especially that any extensive, centres of population grew up in Anglo-Saxon Britain, upon sites chosen by the barbarians. The Romans had colonised and densely populated every suitable spot. The ships' crews of open pirate vessels had no qualities suitable to the founding of a town; and when there is no direct evidence it is always safer of the two conjectures in English topography to believe that any spot which we find inhabited and flourishing in the Anglo-Saxon period, even at its close, was not a town developed during the Dark Ages but one which the pirates, when they first entered the island, had found already inhabited and flourishing, though sometimes perhaps more British than Roman. But though this is always the more historical way of looking at the probable origin of an English town it must be admitted that there is no direct evidence of any town upon the site of Oxford before the Danish invasions, and the first mention of the place by name is as late as eleven years after Alfred's death, when it is recorded that Edward, his son, "took possession of London and of Oxford and of all lands in obedience thereunto."

This first mention, slight as it is, characterises Oxford as being the town of the upper Thames Valley at the opening of the tenth century, and we have what is usually a good basis for history—that is, ecclesiastical tradition and a monastic charter—to show us that a considerable monastery had existed upon the spot for a century and a half before this first mention in the Chronicle.

There still exists in the modern town, to the west of it, a large artificial mound, one of those which have been discovered here and there up and down England, and which are characteristic of a late Saxon method of fortification. Before the advent of the Normans these mounds were defended by palisades only, and were used as but occasional strongholds. It may be conjectured that this Saxon work at Oxford dates from somewhat the same period as does the first mention of the town in the Chronicle. Twelve years later Alfred's grandson is mentioned as dying at Oxford. It may be presumed that his death would indicate the presence of a royal palace. We hear nothing more of this town during the remainder of the tenth century, but we have a long account in what is probably an accurate record of the rising of the townsmen against the Danes in the beginning of the eleventh. The Scandinavians made their last stand in the church of the monastery, and the townsmen burnt it. Five years later a new host of Danes took and burnt the town; and four years later again, Sweyn, in his terrible conquering march, captured it, after very little resistance, in the same year in which he took the crown of England. The brief episode of Edmund Ironside again brings the town into history: he slept here upon his way to London in the late autumn of 1016, and here, very probably, he was killed. From that moment the fortress (as it now certainly was) enters continually into that last anarchy which was only cured by a second advent of European civilisation and the success of its armies at Hastings.

The great national council of 1018, which may be called the settlement of Canute, was held at Oxford, and in 1036 another national council, of even greater importance, which was held to decide upon the succession of Canute's heirs, was again held at Oxford, and it was at Oxford that, four years later, the first Harold died.

Meanwhile, in the near neighbourhood of the city, at Islip, Queen Emma had, half a lifetime earlier, borne a son, who, after the death of all these Danes, remained the legitimate heir to the English throne. Islip was, most probably, not royal, but a private manor of the Queen's, which descended to the Confessor, and it is interesting to note in passing that it was his gift of this land and of its church to Westminster Abbey which originated the present connection between the two—a connection which has now, therefore, behind it nearly nine hundred years of continuity.

In the few hurried months before Hastings the last of the great Anglo-Saxon meetings in the town was summoned. It was held at the end of October, 1065, and was that in which Harold's policy was agreed to. Within twelve months Harold himself was dead, and a victorious invading army was marching upon Wallingford.

In all this record it is clear that Oxford held a continually growing place in the life of England, and especially as a stronghold of whoever might be governing England. What battle was fought there, if any, or how the Normans got it, we do not know, but it is presumed that it suffered in the fighting because the number and value of its houses is given in the subsequent Survey as having fallen very largely indeed.

It is always well, whenever one comes across the Domesday Survey in history, to remember that the whole record is very imperfectly understood. We do not know quite what was being measured: we do not know, for instance, in the case of a town like Oxford, whether all the inhabited houses were counted; or whether only those who by custom gave taxes were counted; nor can we be certain of the meaning of the word vastus, save that it has some connection either with destruction or dilapidation, or lack of occupation, or, possibly, even remission of taxation. But the theory of a sack is not without foundation, for we know that in the case of York (which was certainly sacked by Tostig in 1065 and then again by William in 1068) what is probably a destruction of a similar kind, though a rather greater one, is expressed in similar words.

Whether, however, the number given in the town list of the Conqueror is or is not due to the destruction wrought by the Conquest we must be very careful not to estimate the population of that time upon the basis to-day such a list would afford. The figures of Domesday stand for a much larger population than most historians have hitherto been inclined to grant, as may be shown by considerations to which I shall only allude here, as I shall have to repeat them more fully upon a later page when I speak of urban life upon the Thames. The nomadic element in the life of the early Middle Ages; the smallness of the space allotted for sleeping; the large amount of time spent out of doors; the great proportion of collegiate institutions, not only monastic but military; the life in common which spread as a habit to so many parts of society beyond the monastic; the large families which (from genealogy) we can trust to be as much a character of the early Middle Ages as they, were not the character of the later Middle Ages, the crowd of semi-servile dependants which would be discovered in any large house—all these make us perfectly safe in multiplying by at least ten the number of households counted in the Survey if we would get at the population of those households, and it must be remembered that the houses counted, even in those parts of England which were fairly thoroughly surveyed, can only represent a minimum number, whatever was the method of counting. The lists may in some instances include every single household in a place, though from what we know of the diversity of local custom this is unlikely. In most places it is far more likely that the list covered but some portion that by custom owed a public tax, and this is especially true of the towns.

After Dorchester, which was the first of the fortresses of the Thames, so far as we have any knowledge, and after Oxford, which came next, and appears to have been founded since the beginning of recorded history in these islands, there remain to be considered the other strongholds which held the line of the valley.

It would be easy to multiply these if one were to consider all

77

fortifications whatsoever connected with the general strategic line formed by the Thames, but such a catalogue would exceed the boundaries set to this book. It is proposed to consider only those which were strictly connected with the passage of the stream, and of such there are but three besides Dorchester and Oxford, for that at Cricklade is doubtful, and in any case determines a passage which could be always outflanked upon either side, while the great fortress of the Tower, lying as it does upon the estuarial Thames below bridges, does directly protect a highway.

These three strongholds directly connected with the inland river are Wallingford, Reading and Windsor, and of the three Wallingford and Windsor were more directly military: the last, Reading, appears to have been but an adjunct to a large and civil population; the fourfold quality of Reading in the history of the Thames, as a civil settlement, as a religious centre, as a stronghold, and as one of the very few examples of modern industrial development in the valley, will be considered later. We will take each of the three strongholds in their order down stream.

What determined the importance of Wallingford is not easy to fix nowadays. The explanation more usually given to the great part which this crossing of the Thames played in the early history of Britain is the double one that it was the lowest continuously practicable ford over the river, and that it held the passage of the great road going from London to the west.

Now it is true that any traveller making from London to Bath, or the Mendip Hills, and the lower Severn would, on the whole, find his most direct road to be along the Vale of the White Horse, but the convenience of this line through Wallingford may easily be exaggerated, especially its convenience for men in early times before the valleys were properly drained. Though the ford at Abingdon was more difficult than the ford at Wallingford, yet the line through Abingdon westward along the Farringdon road was certainly shorter than the line through Wantage. Whether the old habit, inherited from pre-historic times, of following the chalk ridge had produced a parallel road just at the foot of that ridge and so had made Wallingford, Wantage, and all the southern edge of the Vale of the White Horse the natural road to the west, or whether it was that the great run of travel ran, when once the Thames had been crossed at Wallingford, slightly south-west towards Bath, it is certain that the Wallingford and Wantage line is the line of travel in early history.

There is no record, and but very little basis for conjecture, as to the origin of the fortifications at Wallingford. Not much is left of them, and though there is some Roman work in the place it is work which has evidently been handled over and over again. It is certainly somewhat late in English history that this "Walled Ford" is heard of—with the tenth century. Its first castle is, of course, Norman, and contemporary with that of Oxford—or rather a year later than that at Oxford, and from the Conquest onward it remains royal. From that time, also, it is perpetually appearing in English history. It was the place of confinement of Edward I. when, as Prince Edward, he was the prisoner of Leicester. It was the attempt to succour that prisoner which led to his removal to Kenilworth, and finally to that escape which permitted him to fight the battle of Evesham. Wallingford passed to Gaveston in Edward the Second's reign, and, remaining continually within the gift of the crown, to the Despenser in the succeeding generation, and finally to Isabella, who declared her policy from within the walls of Wallingford when she returned to the country. It was next held by her favourite, Mortimer, and we afterwards find it, throughout the fourteenth century, a sort of appanage of the heir-apparent, and especially of the Duchy of Cornwall, to which it was attached until the Reformation. It was for a moment under the custody of Chaucer's son: it nursed the childhood of Henry VI., but with the beginning of the next century it had already lost its importance. After half that century had passed the castle was already falling into disrepair; much of the masonry of the town and of the fortress, lying squared and convenient to the river, had been moved down stream for the new buildings at Windsor, and when, nearly a century later again, the Civil War broke out, it was not until after some considerable repair that the place could pretend to stand a siege. It fell to the Parliament, and, before the Restoration, was carefully destroyed, as were throughout England so many foundations of her past by the orders of Oliver Cromwell.

It has often been remarked with surprise that cities and strongholds once densely inhabited and heavily built can disappear and leave no material trace to posterity. That they do so disappear should give pause to those historians who are perpetually using the negative argument, and pretending that the lack of material evidence is sufficient to disturb a strong and early tradition. Those who have watched the process by which abandoned buildings become a quarry will easily understand how all traces of habitation disappear. Three-quarters of what was once Orford, much of what once was Worsted, has gone, and up and down the country-sides to-day one could witness, even in our strictly disciplined civilisation, the removal, by purchase or theft, of abandoned material.

The whole of Wallingford has suffered this fate—the mound, presumably artificial, upon which the first keep stood, and which was, probably, a palisade mound of Anglo-Saxon times, remains, but there is upon it no remaining masonry.

Next down stream of the points with a strategic importance in English history comes Reading. But the strategic importance of Reading was not produced by the town's possessing a site of national moment: it was produced only by local topography. Reading was never (to use a modern term) a "nodal point" in the communications of England.

It may be generally laid down that mere strength of position is noted and greedily seized in barbaric times alone. For mere strength of position is a mere refuge. A strong position (I do not speak, of course, of tactical and temporary, but of permanent, positions), chosen only because it is strong, will save you during a critical short period from the attack of a fierce, unthoughtful, and easily wearied enemy—such as are all barbarians; but it cannot of itself fall into a general scheme of defence, nor, simply because it is strong, intercept the advance of an adversary or support a line of opposition and resistance. Position is always of advantage to a fortress, and, in all but highly civilised times, a necessity—as we shall see when we come to discuss Windsor—but it is not sufficient. A fortress, when society is organised, and when the feud of one small tribe or family against another is not to be feared, derives its principal value from a command of established communications, and established aggregations of power—especially of economic power. Towns alone can feed and house armies; by roads and railways alone can armies proceed.

There are, indeed, examples of a chain of positions so striking that, from their strength alone, a strategic line imposes itself; but these are very rare. Another, and much commoner, exception to the rule I have stated is the growth of what was once a barbaric stronghold, chosen merely for its position, into a larger centre of population, through which communications necessarily lead, and in which stores and other opportunities for armies can be provided. Such places often preserve a continuity of strategic importance, from civilised, through barbaric, to civilised times again. Laon is an excellent instance of this, and so is Constantine another, and so is Luxembourg a third—indeed they are numerous.

But, in spite of—or, rather, as is proved by—these exceptions the fortresses of an organised people are found at the conjunction of their communications, or at places (such as straits or passes) which have the monopoly of communication, or they are identical with great aggregations of population and opportunity, or at least they are situated in spots from which such aggregations can be commanded. Position is always of value, but only as an adjunct.

Now Reading, save, perhaps, in barbaric times, when the Thames was the main highway of Southern England, occupied no such vantage until the nineteenth century. To-day, with its large population, its provision of steam and electrical power, and above all, its command of the main junction between the southern and middle railways, Reading would again prove of primary strategic importance if we still considered warfare with our equals as a possibility. But during all previous centuries, since the Dark Ages, Reading was potentially, as it is still actually, civilian; and, indeed, it is as the typical great town of the Thames Valley that it will be treated later in these pages.

The long and narrow peninsula between the Kennet and the Thames was an ideal place for defence. It needed but a trench from the one marsh to the other to secure the stronghold. But though this was evident to every fighter, though it is as such a stronghold that Reading is mentioned first in history, yet the advantage was never permanently held. Armies hold Reading, fall back on the town, fight near it, and raid it: but it is never a great fortress in the intervals of wars, because, while Oxford commanded the Drovers' Road, Wallingford the western road, and Windsor (as we shall see in a moment) London itself, Reading neither held a line of supply nor an accumulation of supply, and was, therefore, civilian, though it was nearly as easy to hold as Windsor, as easy as Dorchester, its parallel, easier than Oxford, and far easier than Wallingford, which had, indeed, no natural defences whatsoever.

Proceeding with the stream, there is no further stronghold till we come to Windsor.

Even to-day, and in an England that has lost hold of her past more than has any rival nation, Windsor seems to the passer-by to possess a meaning. That hill of stones, sharp though most of its modern outlines are, set upon another hill for a pedestal, gives, even to a modern patriot, a hint of history; and when it is seen from up-stream, showing its only noble part, where the Middle Ages still linger, it has an aspect almost approaching majesty.

The creator of Windsor was the Conqueror. The artificial mound on which the Round Tower stands may or may not be pre-historic. The slopes of the hill were inhabited, like nearly all our English sites, by the Romans, and by the savages before and after the Romans; but the welter of the Saxon dark ages did not use this abrupt elevation for a stronghold. What military reasoning led William of Falaise to discern it at once and there to build his keep?

In order to answer that question let us consider what other points in the valley were at his disposal.

Reading we have discussed. The chalk spurs in the gorge by

Goring and Pangbourne are not isolated (as is that of Chateau Gaillard, for instance), and are dominated by the neighbouring heights. The escarpment opposite Henley offered a good site for an eleventh-century castle—but the steep cliff of Windsor had this advantage beyond all the others—that it was at exactly the right distance from London. Windsor is the warden of the capital.

If the reader will look at a modern geological map, he will see from Wallingford to Bray a great belt of chalk in which the trench of the Thames is carved. Alluvials and gravels naturally flank the stream, but chalk is the ground rock of the whole. To the west and to the east of this belt he will notice two curious isolated patches, detached from the main body of the chalk. That to the west forms the twin height of the Sinodun Hills, rising abruptly out of the green sand; that to the east is the knoll of Windsor, rising abruptly out of the thick and damp clay. It is a singular and unique patch, almost exactly round, and as a result of some process at which geology can hardly guess the circle is bisected by the river. If ever the chalk of the north bank rose high it has, in some manner, been worn down. That on the south bank remains in a steep cliff with which everyone who uses the river is familiar. It was the summit of this chalk hill piercing through the clays that the Conqueror noted for his purpose, and he was, to repeat, determined (we must presume) by the distance from London.

The command of a great town, especially a metropolis, is but partially effected by a fortress situated within its limits. In case of a popular revolt, and still more in case the resources of the town are held by an enemy, such a fortress will be penned in and find itself suffering a siege far more rigorous than any that could be laid in an open country-side. On this account the urban fortresses of the Middle Ages are to be found (at least in large cities) lying upon an extreme edge of the walls and reposing, as far as possible, upon uninhabited land or upon water, or both. The two classic examples of this rule are, of course, the Tower and the Louvre, each standing down stream, just outside the wall, and each reposing on the river.

But in an active time even this precaution fails, and that for two reasons. First, the growth of the town makes any possible garrison of the fortress too small for the force with which it might have to cope; and, secondly, this same growth physically overlaps the exterior fortress; suburbs grow up beyond the wall, and the castle finds itself at last embedded in the town. Thus within a hundred and fifty years of its completion the Louvre was but a residence, wholly surrounded, save upon the water front, by the packed houses within the new wall of Marcel.

A tendency therefore arises, more or less early according to

82

local circumstance, to establish a fortified base within striking distance of the civilian centre which it is proposed to command; and striking distance is a day's march. The strict alliance between Paris and the Crown forbade such an experiment to the Capetian Monarchy, but, even in that case, the truth of the general military proposition involved is proved by the power which Montlhéry possessed until the middle of the twelfth century of doing mischief to Paris. In the case of London, and of a population the wealthier of whom were probably for some years hostile to the Conqueror, the immediate necessity for an exterior base presented itself, and though the distance from London was indeed considerable, Windsor, under the circumstances of that moment, proved the most suitable point at which to establish the fortress.

Some centuries earlier or later the exact point for fortification would have lain at Staines, and Windsor may be properly regarded as a sort of second best to Staines.

The great Roman roads continued until the twelfth century to be the main highways of the barbaric and mediæval armies. We know, for instance, from a charter of Westminster's, that Oxford Street was called, in the last years of the Saxon Dynasty, "Via Militaria," and it was this road which was still in its continuation the marching road upon London from the south and west: from Winchester, which was still in a fashion the capital of England and the seat of the Treasury. Now Staines marks the spot where this road crossed the river. It was a "nodal point," commanding at once the main approach to London by land and the main approach by water.

But there is more than this in favour of Staines. I have already said that a fortress commanding a civilian population—an ancient fortress, at least—can do so with the best effect at the distance of an easy march. Now Staines is not seventeen miles from Tyburn, and a good road all the way: Windsor is over twenty, and for the last miles there was no good, hard road in the time of its foundation.

But, though Staines had all these advantages, it was rejected from a lack of position. Position was still of first importance, and remained so till the seventeenth century. The new Castle, like so many hundred others built by the genius of the same race, must stand on a steep hill even if the choice of such a site involved a long, instead of a reasonable, day's march. Windsor alone offered that opportunity, and, standing isolated upon the chalk, beyond the tide, accessible by water and by road, became to London what, a hundred years later, Chateau Gaillard was to become for a brief space to Rouen.

The choice was made immediately after the Conquest. In the

course of the Dark Ages whatever Roman farms clustered here had dwindled, the Roman cemetery was abandoned, the original name of the district forgotten, and the Saxon "Winding Shore" grew up at Old Windsor, two or three miles down stream. Old Windsor was not a borough, but it was a very considerable village. It paid dues to its lords to the amount of some twenty-five loads of corn and more—say 100 quarters—and it had at least 100 houses, since that number is set down in Domesday, and, as we have previously said, Domesday figures necessarily express a minimum. We may take it that its population was something in the neighbourhood of 1000.

This considerable place was under the lordship of the abbots of Westminster. It had been a royal manor when Edward the Confessor came to the throne; he gave it to his new great abbey. When the Conqueror needed the whole neighbourhood for his new purpose he exchanged it against land in Essex, which he conveyed to the abbey, and he added (for the manorial system was still flexible) half a hide from Clewer on the west side of the Windsor territory. This half-hide gave him his approach to the platform of chalk on which he designed to build.

He began his work quickly. Within four years of Hastings, and long before the conquest of the Saxon aristocracy was complete, he held his Court at Windsor and summoned a synod there, and, though we do not know when the keep was completed, we can conjecture, from the rapidity with which all Norman work was done, that the walls were defensible even at that time. Of his building perhaps nothing remains. The forest to the south, with its opportunities for hunting, and the increasing importance of London (which was rapidly becoming the capital of England) made Windsor of greater value than ever in the eyes of his son. Henry I. rebuilt or greatly enlarged the castle, lived in it, was married in it, and accomplished in it the chief act of his life, when he caused fealty to be sworn to his daughter, Matilda, and prepared the advent of the Angevin. When the civil wars were over, and the treaty between Henry II. and Stephen was signed, Windsor ("Mota de Windsor"), though it does not seem to have stood a siege, was counted the second fortress of the realm.

Of the exact place of Windsor in mediæval strategy, of its relations to London and to Staines, and all we have just mentioned, as also of the great importance of cavalry in the Middle Ages, no better example can be quoted than the connected episode of April-June 1215, which may be called—to give it a grandiose name—the Campaign of Magna Charta. It further illustrates points which should never be forgotten in the reading of early English history, though they are too particular for the general purpose of this book—

to wit, the way in which London increased in military value throughout the twelfth and thirteenth centuries; the strategic importance of the few old national roads as late as the reign of John, and that power of the defensive, even in the field, which made general and strategic, as opposed to tactical, attack so cautious, decisive action so rare, and when it was decisive, so thorough.

This book is no place wherein to develop a theme which history will confirm with regard to the aristocratic revolt against the vice and the genius of the third Plantagenet. The strategy of the quarrel alone concerns us.

When John's admirable diplomacy had failed (as diplomacy will under the test of arms), and when his Continental allies had been crushed at Bouvines in the summer of 1214, the rebels in England found their opportunity. The great lords, especially those of the north, took oath in the autumn to combine. The accounts of this conspiracy are imperfect, but its general truth may be accepted. John, who from this moment lay perpetually behind walls, held a conference in the Temple during the January of 1215—to be accurate, upon the Epiphany of that year—and he struck a compact with the conspirators that there should be a truce between their forces and those of the Crown until Low Sunday—which fell that year upon the 26th of April. The great nobles, mistrusting his faith with some justice (especially as he had taken the Cross), gathered their army some ten days before the expiry of the interval, but, as befitted men who claimed in especial to defend the Catholic Church · and its principles, they were scrupulous not to engage in actual fighting before the appointed day. The size of this army we cannot tell, but as it contained from 2000 to 3000 armed and mounted gentlemen it must have counted at least double that tale of cavalry, and perhaps five-, perhaps ten-fold the number of foot soldiers. A force of 15,000 to 30,000 men in an England of some 5,000,000 (I more than double the conventional figures) was prepared to enforce feudal independence against the central government, even at the expense of ceding vast territories to Scotland or of submitting to the nominal rule of a foreign king. Against this army the King had a number of mercenaries, mainly drawn from his Continental possessions, probably excellent soldiers, but scattered among the numerous garrisons which it was his titular office to defend.

In the last days of the truce the rebels marched to Brackley and encamped there on Low Monday—the 27th April. The choice of the site should be noted. It lies in a nexus of several old marching roads. The Port Way, a Roman road from Dorchester northward, the Watling Street all lay within half-an-hour's ride. The King was at Oxford, a day's march away. They negotiated with him, and their claims were refused, yet they did not attack him (though his force was small), partly because the function of government was still with him and partly because the defensive power of Oxford was great. They wisely preferred the nearest of his small official garrisons-that holding the castle of Northampton. They approached it up the Roman road through Towcester. They failed before it after two weeks of effort, and marched on to the next royal post at Bedford, which was by far the nearest of the national garrisons. It was betrayed to them. When they were within the gates they received a message from the wealthier citizens of London (who were in practice one with the Feudal Oligarchy), begging them to enter the capital.

What followed could only have been accomplished: by cavalry, by cavalry in high training, by a force under excellent generalship, and by one whose leaders appreciated the all-importance of London in the coming struggle. The rebels left Bedford immediately, marched all that day, all the succeeding night, and early on the Sunday morning, 24th May, entered London, and by the northern gate. Their entry was not even challenged.

From Bedford to St. Paul's is—as the crow flies—between forty and fifty miles: whatever road a man may take would make it nearer fifty than forty. Bearing, as did this army, towards the east until it struck the Ermine Street, the whole march must have been well over fifty miles.

This fine feat was not a barren one: it was well worth the effort and loss which it must have cost. London could feed, recruit, and remount an army of even this magnitude with ease. The Tower was held by a royal garrison, but it could do nothing against so great a town.

From London, as though the name of the city had a sort of national authority, the Barons, who now felt themselves to be hardly rebels but almost co-equals in a civil war, issued letters of mandate to others of their class and to their inferiors. These letters were obeyed, not perhaps without some hesitation, but at any rate with a final obedience which turned the scale against the King. John was now in a very distinct inferiority, and even of his personal attendants a considerable number left the Court on learning of the defection of London. In all this long struggle nothing but the occupation of the capital had proved enough to make John feign a compromise. As excellent an intriguer as he was a fighter he asked nothing better than to hear once more the terms of the Barons.

He proceeded to Windsor, asked for a parley, issued a safeguard to the emissaries of the Barons, and despatched this document upon the 8th June, giving it a validity of three days. His enemies waited somewhat longer, perhaps in order to collect the more distant contingents, and named Runnymede—a pasture upon the right bank of the Thames just above Staines—as the place of meeting.

There are those who see in the derivation of the name "Runnymede" an ancient use of the meadow as a place of council. This is, of course, mere conjecture, but at any rate it was, at this season of the year, a large, dry field, in which a considerable force could encamp. The Barons marched along the old Roman military road, which is still the high-road to Staines from London, crossed the river, and encamped on Runnymede. Here the Charta was presented, and probably, though not certainly, signed and sealed. The local tradition ascribes the site of the actual signature to "Magna Charta" island—an eyot just up-stream from the field, now called Runnymede, but neither in tradition nor in recorded history can this detail be fixed with any exactitude. The Charta is given as from Runnymede upon the 15th June, and for the purpose of these pages what we have to note is that these two months of marching and fighting had ended upon the strategic point of Staines, and had clearly shown its relation to Windsor and to London.

In the short campaign that followed, during which John so very nearly recovered his power, the capital importance of Windsor reappears. Louis of France, to whom the Barons were willing to hand over what was left of order in England, had occupied all the south and west, including even Worcester, and, of course, London. In this occupation the exception of Dover, which the French were actively besieging, must be regarded as an isolated point, but Windsor, which John's men held against the allies, threw an angle of defence right down into the midst of the territory lost to the Crown. Windsor was, of course, besieged; but John's garrison, holding out as it did, saved the position. The King was at Wallingford at one moment during the siege; his proximity tempted the enemy to raise the siege, to leave Windsor in the hands of the royal garrison, and to advance against him, or rather to cut him off in his advance eastward. They marched with the utmost rapidity to Cambridge, but John was ahead of them: and before they could return to the capture of Windsor he was rapidly confirming his power in the north and the east.

It must not be forgotten in all this description that Windsor was helped in its development as a fortress by the presence to the south of the hill of a great space of waste lands.

These waste lands of Western Europe, which it was impossible or unprofitable to cultivate, were, by a sound political tradition, vested in the common authority, which was the Crown.

Indeed they still remain so vested in most European countries. The Cantons of Switzerland, the Communes and the National Governments of France, Italy, and Spain remain in possession of the waste. It is only with us that wealthy private owners have been permitted to rob the Commonwealth of so obvious an inheritance, a piece of theft which they have accomplished with complete cynicism, and by specific acts whose particular dates can be quoted, though historians are very naturally careful to leave the process but vaguely analysed. Indeed, the last and most valuable of these waste spaces, the New Forest itself, might have entirely disappeared had not Charles I. (the last king in England to attempt a repression of the landed class) so forcibly urged the local engrosser to disgorge as to compel him, with Hampden and the rest, to a burning zeal for political liberty.

This great waste space to the south of Windsor Hill became, after the Conquest, the Forest, and apart from the hunting which it afforded to the Royal palace, served a certain purpose on the military side as well.

To develop a thought which has already been touched on in these pages, mediæval fortification was dual in character: it had either a purely strategical object, in which case the site was chosen with an eye to its military value, whether inhabited or not, or the stronghold or fortification was made to develop an already existing town or site of importance. Of the second sort was Wallingford, but of the first sort, as we have seen, was Windsor. Indeed the distinction is normal to all fortification and exists upon the Continent to-day. For instance, the first-class fortress Paris is an example of the second sort, the first-class fortress Toul of the first. Again, all German fortresses, without exception, are of the second sort, while all Swiss fortification, what little of it exists, is of the first.

Now where the first category is concerned a waste space is of value, though its dimensions will vary in military importance according to the means of communication of the time. A stronghold may be said to repose upon that side through which communications are most difficult.

It is true that this space lying to the south of Windsor was of no very great dimensions, but such as it was, uninhabited and therefore unprovided with stores of any kind, it prevented surprise from the south.

The next point of strategic importance on the Thames, and the last, is the Tower.

Though it is below bridges it must fall into the scheme of this book, because its whole military history and connection with the

88

story of England is bound up with the inland and not with the estuarial river.

It was, as has already been pointed out, one long day's march from Windsor—a march along the old Roman road from Staines. This land passage more than halved the distance by river, it cut off not only the numerous large turns which the Thames begins to take between Middlesex and Surrey, but also the general sweep southward of the river, and it avoided, what another road might have necessitated, the further crossing of the stream.

Long as the march is, there was no fortification of importance between one point and the other, and mediæval history is crammed with instances of armies leaving the Tower to march to Windsor in one day, or leaving Windsor to march to the Tower.

The position of the Tower we saw in an earlier page to be due to the same geographical causes as had built up so many of the urban strongholds of Europe. It was situated upon the very bank of the river which fed the capital, it was down stream from the town, and it was just outside the walls. In a word, it was the parallel of the Louvre.

Its remote origins are doubtful; some have imagined that they are Roman, and that if not in the first part of the Roman occupation at least towards the end of those wealthy and populous three centuries, which are the foundation and the making of England, some fortification was built on the brow of the little eminence which here slopes down to the high-water mark.

I will quote the evidence, such as it is, and the reader will perceive how difficult it is to arrive at a conclusion.

Of actual Roman remains all we have is a couple of coins of the end of the fourth century (probably minted at Constantinople), a silver ingot of the same period, and a funeral inscription. No indubitably Roman work has been discovered.

On the other hand there has been no modern investigation of those foundations of the White Tower where, if anywhere, Roman work might be expected. This exhausts the direct evidence. In sciences such as geology or the criticism of Sacred Books evidence to this extent would be ample to overset the firmest traditions or the most self-evident conclusion of common human experience. But history is bound to a greater caution, and it must be reluctantly admitted that the two coins, the ingot and the bit of stone are insufficient to prove the existence of a Roman fortress.

Leaving such material and direct evidence we have the tradition, which is a fairly strong one, of Roman fortification here, and we have the analogy, so frequently occurring in space and time throughout the history and the area of Western Europe, that Gaul reproduces Rome. What the Conqueror saw (it might be vaguely argued) to be the strategical position for London, that a Roman emperor would have seen. But against this argument from tradition, which is fairly strong, and that argument from analogy, which is weak, we have other and contrary considerations.

Rome even in her decline did not build her citadels outside the walls: that was a habit which grew up in the Dark and early Middle Ages, and was attached to the differentiation between the civic and military aspects of the State.

Again, Roman fortification of every kind is connected with earthworks. So far as we can tell from recorded history the ditch round the Tower was not dug till the end of the twelfth century. Finally, there is this strong argument against the theory of a Roman origin to the Tower that had such a Roman fortress existed an extension of the town would almost certainly have gathered round it.

One of the features of the break-up of Roman society was the enormous expansion of the towns. We have evidence of it on every side and nowhere more than in Northern Africa. This expansion took place everywhere, but especially and invariably in the presence of a garrison, and indeed the military conditions of the fourth century, with its cosmopolitan and partially hereditary army, fixed in permanent garrisons and forming as it were a local caste, presupposed a large dependent civilian population at the very gates of the camp or stronghold. Thus you have the Palatine suburb to the south of Lutetia right up against the camp, and Verecunda just outside Lamboesis. Now there is nothing of the sort in the neighbourhood of the Tower. It seems certain that from the earliest times London ended here cleanly at the wall, and that except along the Great Eastern Road the neighbourhood of the Tower was agricultural land.

How then could a tradition have arisen with regard to Roman occupation? It is but a conjecture, though a plausible one, that when the pirate raids grew in severity this knoll down stream was fortified, while still the ruling class was Latin speaking and while still the title of Cæsar was familiar, whether before or after the withdrawal of the Legions. If this were the case, then, on the analogy of other similar sites, one may imagine something like the following: that in the Dark Ages the masonry was used as a quarry for other constructions, that the barbarians would occasionally stockade the site, though not permanently, and only for the purposes of their ephemeral but constant quarrels; and one may suggest that when the barbaric period was ended, by the landing of William's army, the place was still, by a tradition now six hundred years old, a public area under the control of the Crown and one such as would lend itself to the design of a permanent fortification. William, finding it in this condition, erected upon it the great keep which was to be the last of his fortifications along the line of the river, and the pivot for the control of London.

This keep is of course the White Tower, which still impresses even our generation with the squat and square shoulders of Norman strength. It and Ely are the best remaining expressions of the hardy little men, and it fills one, as does everything Norman, from the Tyne to the Euphrates, with something of awe. This building, the White Tower, is the Tower itself; the rest is but an accretion, partly designed for defence, but latterly more for habitation. Its name of the "White" Tower is probably original, though we do not actually find the term "La Blaunche Tour" till near the middle of the fourteenth century. The presumption that it is the original name is founded upon a much earlier record—namely, that of 1241, in which not only is it ordered that the tower be repainted white, but in which mention is also made that its original colour had been "worn by the weather and by the long process of time." Such a complaint would take one back to the twelfth century, and quite probably to the first building of the Keep. The object of whitening the walls of the Tower is again explicable by the very reasonable conjecture that it would so serve as a landmark over the long, flat stretches of the lower river. It was the last conspicuous building against the mass of the great town, and there are many examples of similar landmarks used at the head of estuaries or sea passages. When these are not spires they are almost invariably white, especially where they are so situated as to catch the southern or the eastern sun.

The exact date at which the plan was undertaken we do not know, but it is obviously one with the scheme of building Windsor, and must date from much the same period. The order to build was given by the Conqueror to the Bishop of Rochester, Gundulph. Now Gundulph was not promoted to the See of Rochester till 1077. Exactly twenty years later, in 1097, the son of the Conqueror built the outer wall. The Keep was then presumed to be completed, and at some time during those twenty years it must have been begun, probably about 1080. That which we have seen increasing, the military importance of Windsor, diminished the military importance of the Tower, until, with the close of the Middle Ages, it had become no more than a prison. It was not indeed swamped by the growth of the town, as was its parallel the Louvre, but the increase of wealth (and therefore of the means of war), coupled with the correspondingly increased population, made both urban fortresses increasingly difficult to hold as mediæval civilisation developed.

The whole history of the Tower is the history of military misfortune, which grows as London expands in numbers and prosperity. It probably held out under Mandeville when the Londoners (who were always the allies of the aristocracy against the national government) besieged it under the civil wars of Stephen; but even so there was bad luck attached to it, for when Mandeville was taken prisoner he was compelled to sign its surrender. Within a generation Longchamp again surrendered it to the young Prince John; he was for the moment leading the aristocracy, which, when it was his turn to reign, betrayed him. It was surrendered to the baronial party by the King as a trust or pledge for the execution of Magna Charta, and though it was put into the hands of the Archbishop, who was technically neutral, it was from that moment the symbol of a successful rebellion, as it had already proved to be in the past and was to prove so often again.

It was handed over to Louis of France upon his landing, and during the next reign almost every misfortune of Henry III. is connected with the Tower. He was perpetually taking refuge in it, holding his Court in it: losing it again, as the rebels succeeded, and regaining it as they failed. This long and unfortunate tenure of his is illumined only by one or two delightful phrases which one cannot but retain as one reads. Thus there is the little written order, which still remains to us for the putting of painted windows into the Chapel of St John, the northern one of which was to have for its design "some little Mary or other, holding her Child"—"quandam Mariolam tenenten puerum suum." There is also a very pleasing legend in the same year, 1241, when the fall of certain new buildings was ascribed to the action of St. Thomas, who was seen by a priest in a dream upsetting them with his crozier and saying that he did this "as a good citizen of London, because these new buildings were not put up for the defence of the realm but to overawe the town," and he added this charming remark: "If I had not undertaken the duty myself St. Edward or another would have done it."

Even when Henry's misfortunes were at an end, and when the Battle of Evesham was won, the Tower was perpetually unfortunate. A body of rebels surrounded it, and in the defence were present a great number of Jews, who had fled from the fighting in the city only to find themselves pressed for service in defence of the fortress. From that moment they make no further appearance in English military history till the South African War, unless indeed their appearance in chains thirteen years later in this same Tower as prisoners for financial trickery can be counted a military event.

Upon this occasion the siege was raised by the promptitude and energy of Prince Edward—the man who as King was to march to Cærnarvon and to the Grampians had already in his boyhood shown the energy and the military aptitude of his grandfather King John. He was but twenty years old, yet he had already done all the fighting at Lewes, he had already won Evesham, and now, at the end of spring, he made one march from Windsor to the Tower and relieved it. It was almost the last time that the Tower stood for the success of authority. From this time onwards it is, as it had been before, the unfortunate symbol of successful rebellion. Edward II. had to leave it in his fatal year of 1326, the Londoners poured in and incidentally massacred the Bishop of Exeter, into whose hands it had been entrusted.

In 1460 it surrendered to the House of York, and from that time onwards becomes more and more of a prison and less and less of a fortress.

The preponderatingly military aspect of the Thames Valley in English history dwindles with the dwindling of military energy in our civilisation, and passes with the passing of a governing class that was military rather than commercial.

Sites which owed their importance to strategical position, and which had hence grown into considerable towns, ceased to show any but a civilian character, and even in the only episode of consequence wherein fighting occurred in England since the Middle Ages—the episode of the Civil Wars—the banks of the Thames, though perpetually infested by either army, saw very little serious fighting, and that although the line of the Thames was the critical line of action during the first stage of the war.

For the Civil Wars as a whole were but an affair upon the flank of the general struggle in Europe: the losses were never heavy, and in the first stages one can hardly call it fighting at all.

The losses at the skirmish of Edge Hill were, indeed, respectable, though most of them seem to have been incurred after the true fighting ceased, but with that exception, and especially upon the line of the Thames itself, the losses were extraordinarily small.

One may say that Oxford and London were the two objective points of the opposing forces from the close of 1642 to the spring of 1644. The King's Government at Oxford, the Parliament in London, were the civil bases, at least, upon which the opposing forces pivoted, and the two intermediate points were Abingdon and Reading. To read the contemporary, and even the modern, history of the time, one would imagine from the terms used that these places were the theatre of considerable military operations. We hear, with every technicality which the Continental struggle had rendered familiar to Englishmen, of sieges, assaults, headquarters, and even hornworks. But when one looks at dates and figures it is not easy to treat the matter seriously. Here, for instance, is Abingdon, within a short walk of Oxford, and the Royalists easily allow it to be occupied by Essex in the spring of '44. Even so Abingdon is not used as a base for doing anything more serious than "molesting" the university town. And it was so held that Rupert tried to recapture it, of all things in the world, with cavalry! He was "overwhelmed" by the vastly superior forces of the enemy, and his attempt failed. When one has thoroughly grasped this considerable military event one next learns that the overwhelming forces were a trifle over a thousand in number!

Next an individual gentleman with a few followers conceives the elementary idea of blocking the western road at Culham Bridge, and isolating Abingdon upon this side. He begins building a "fort." A certain proportion of the handful in Abingdon go out and kill him and the fort is not proceeded with: and so forth. A military temper of this sort very easily explains the cold-blooded massacre of prisoners which the Parliament permitted, and which has given to the phrase "Abingdon Law" the unpleasant flavour which it still retains.

The story of Reading in the earlier part of the struggle is much the same. Reading was held as a royal garrison and fortified in '43. According to the garrison the fortification was contemptible, according to the procedures it was of the most formidable kind. Indeed they doubted whether it could be captured by an assault of less than 5000 men, a number which appeared at this stage of the campaign so appalling that it is mentioned as a sort of standard of comparison with the impossible. The garrison surrendered just as relief was approaching it, and after a strain which it had endured for no less than ten days; but the capture of Reading was not effected entirely without bloodshed; certainly fifty men were killed (counting both sides), possibly a few more; and the whole episode is a grotesque little foot-note to the comic opera upon which rose the curtain of the Civil Wars. It was not till the appearance of Cromwell, with his highly paid and disciplined force, that the tragedy began.

Even after Cromwell had come forward as the chief leader, in fact if not in name, the apparent losses are largely increased by the random massacres to which his soldiers were unfortunately addicted. Thus after Naseby a hundred women were killed for no particular reason except that killing was in the air, and similarly after Philiphaugh the conscience of the Puritans forbade them to keep their word to the prisoners they had taken, who were put to the sword in cold blood: the women, however, on this occasion, were drowned.

After the Civil Wars all the military meaning of the Thames disappears. Nor is it likely to revive short of a national disaster; but that disaster would at once teach us the strategical meaning of this great highway running through the south of England with its attendant railways, it would re-create the strategical value of the point where the Thames turns northward and where its main railways bifurcate; it would provide in several conceivable cases, as it provided to Charles I. and to William III., the line of approach on London.

\* \* \* \* \*

So far as we have considered the Thames, first as a line of pre-historic settlements, passing successively into the Roman, the barbaric and the Norman phases of our history; and secondly, as a field on which one can plot out certain strategical points and show how these points created the original importance of the towns which grew about them.

In the next part of these notes I propose to consider the economic or civil development of the Thames above London, and to show how the foundations of its permanent prosperity was laid. That economic phenomenon has at its roots the action of the Benedictine Order. It was the great monasteries which bridged the transition between Rome and the Dark Ages throughout North-Western Europe; it was they that recovered land wasted by the barbarian invasions, and that developed heaths and fens which the Empire even in its maturity had never attempted to exploit.

The effect of the barbarian invasions was different in different provinces of the Roman Empire, though roughly speaking it increased in intensity with the distance from Rome. It is probable that the actual numbers of the barbarian invaders was small even in Britain, as it certainly was in Northern Gaul, but we must not judge of the effect produced upon civilisation by this catastrophe, as though it were a mere question of numbers. So large a proportion of the population was servile, and so fixed had the imagination of everyone become in the idea that the social order was eternal; so entirely had the army become a professional thing, and probably a thing of routine divorced from the civilian life round it, that at the close of the fourth century a little shock from without was enough to produce a very considerable result. In Eastern Britain, small as the number of the invaders must necessarily have been, religion itself

95

was almost, if not entirely, destroyed, and the whole fabric of Roman civilisation appears to have dissolved—with the exception, of course, of such irremovable things as the agricultural system, the elements of municipal life, and the simpler arts. Even the language very probably changed in the eastern part of the island, and passed from what we may conceive to have been Low Latin in the towns and Celtic dialects in the country-sides, with possibly Teutonic settlements here and there along the eastern shore, to a generally confused mass of Teutonic dialects scattered throughout the eastern and northern half of the island and enclosing but isolated fragments of Celtic speech.

So far as we can judge the disaster was complete, but it was destined that Britain should be recivilised.

St Augustine landed, and after the struggle of the seventh century between those petty chieftains who sympathised with, and those who opposed, the order of cultivated European life, the battle was won in favour of that civilisation which we still enjoy. It would have been impossible to re-create a sound agriculture and to refound the arts and learning; especially would it have been impossible to refound the study of letters, upon which all material civilisation depends, had it not been for the monastic institution. This institution did more work in Britain than in any other province of the Empire. And it had far more to do. It found a district utterly wrecked, perhaps half depopulated, and having lost all but a vague memory of the old Roman order; it had to remake, if it could, of all this part of a Europe. No other instrument was fitted for the purpose.

The chief difficulty of starting again the machine of civilisation when its parts have been distorted by a barbarian interlude, whether external or internal in origin, is the accumulation of capital. The next difficulty is the preservation of such capital in the midst of continual petty feuds and raids, and the third is that general continuity of effort, and that treasuring up of proved experience, to which a barbaric time, succeeding upon the decline of a civilisation, is particularly unfitted. For the surmounting of all these difficulties the monks of Western Europe were suited to a high degree. Fixed wealth could be accumulated in the hands of communities whose whole temptation was to gather, and who had no opportunity for spending in waste. The religious atmosphere in which they grew up forbade their spoliation, at least in the internal wars of a Christian people, and each of the great foundations provided a community of learning and treasuring up of experience which single families, especially families of barbaric chieftains, could never have achieved. They provided leisure for literary effort, and a strict disciplinary rule enforcing regular, continuous, and assiduous labour, and they provided these in a society from which exact application of such a kind had all but disappeared.

The monastic institution, so far as Western Europe was concerned, was comparatively young when the work in Britain was begun. The fifth century had seen its inception; it was still embryonic in the sixth; the seventh, which was the date of its great conquest of the English country-sides, was for it a period of youth and of vigour as fresh as was, let us say, the thirteenth century for the renaissance of civil learning. We must not think of these early foundations as we think of the complicated, wealthy, somewhat restricted and privileged bodies of the later Middle Ages. They were all more or less of one type, and that type a simple one. They all sprang from the same Benedictine stem. It was the quality of all to be somewhat independent in management, and especially to work in large units, and out of the very many which sprang, up all over the island three particularly concern the Thames Valley. Each of them dates from the very beginnings of Anglo-Saxon history, each of them has its roots in legend, and each of them continued for close upon a thousand years to be a capital economic centre of English life. These three great Benedictine foundations are WESTMINSTER, CHERTSEY, and ABINGDON.

When civilisation returned in fulness with the Norman Conquest, another great house of the first importance was founded—at Reading; and, much later, a fourth at Sheen. To these we shall turn in their place, as also to the string of dependent houses and small foundations which line the river almost from its source right down to London: indeed the only type of religious foundation which historic notes such as these can afford to neglect is the monastery or nunnery built in a town, and for the purposes of a town, after the civic life of a town had developed. These very numerous houses (most numerous, of course, in Oxford), such as the Observants of Richmond and a host of others, do not properly enter into the scheme we are considering. They are not causes but effects of the development of civilisation in the Thames Valley.

Abingdon, Westminster, and Chertsey are all ascribed by tradition, and each by a very vital and well-documented tradition, to the seventh century: Abingdon and Chertsey to its close; Westminster, with less assurance, to its beginning. All three, we may take it, did arise in that period which was for the eastern part of this island a time when all the work of Europe had to be begun again. Though we know nothing of the progress of the Saxon pirates in the province of Britain, and though history is silent for the hundred and fifty years covered by the disaster, yet on the analogy

97

of other and later raids from the North Sea we may imagine that no inland part of the country suffered more than the valley of the Thames. All that was left of the Roman order, wealth and right living, must have appeared at the close of that sixth century, when the Papal Mission landed, something as appears the wrecked and desolate land upon the retirement of a flood. To cope with such conditions, to reintroduce into the ravaged and desecrated province, which had lost its language in the storm, all its culture, and even its religion, a new beginning of energy and of production, came, with the peculiar advantages we have seen it to possess for such a work, the monastic institution. For two centuries the great houses were founded all over England: their attachment to Continental learning, their exactitude, their corporate power of action, were all in violent contrast to, and most powerfully educational for, the barbarians in the midst of whom they grew. It may be truly said that if we regard the life of England as beginning anew with the Saxon invasion, if that disaster of the pirate raids be considered as so great that it offers a breach of continuity in the history of Britain, then the new country which sprang up, speaking Teutonic dialects, and calling itself by its present name of England, was actually created by the Benedictine monks.

It was within a very few years of St. Augustine's landing that Westminster must have been begun. There are several versions of the story: the most detailed statement we have ascribes it to the particular year 604, but varied as are the forms in which the history, or rather the legend, is preserved, the truth common to all is the foundation quite early in the seventh century. It was very probably supported by what barbaric Government there was in London at the time and initiated, moreover, according to one form of the legend, and that not the least plausible, by the first bishop of the see. The site was at the moment typical of all those which the great monasteries of the West were to turn from desert places to gardens: it was a waste tract of ground called "Thorney," lying low, triangular in shape, bounded by the two reedy streams that descended through the depression which now runs across the Green Park and Mayfair, and emptied themselves into the Thames, the one just above, the other 100 or 200 yards below, the site of the Houses of Parliament.

The moment the foundation was established a stream of wealth tended towards it: it was at the very gate of the largest commercial city in the kingdom and it was increasingly associated, as the Anglo-Saxon monarchy developed, with the power of the Central Government. This process culminated in the great donation and rebuilding of Edward the Confessor.

The period of this new endowment was one well chosen to

launch the future glory of Westminster. England was all prepared to be permeated with the Norman energy, and when immediately after the Conquest came, the great shrine inherited all the glamour of a lost period, while it established itself with the new power as a sort of symbol of the continuity of the Crown. There William was anointed, there was his palace and that of his son. When, with the next century, the seat of Government became fixed, and London was finally established as the capital, Westminster had already become the seat of the monarchy.

Chertsey, next up the river, took on the work. Like Westminster—though, by tradition, a few years later than Westminster—its foundation goes back to the birth of England. Its history is known in some detail, and is full of incident, so that it may be called the pivot upon which, presumably, turned the development of the Thames Valley above London for two hundred years. Its site is worth noting. The rich, but at first probably swampy, pasturage upon the Surrey side was just such a position as one foundation after another up and down England settled on. To reclaim land of this kind was one of the special functions of the great abbeys, and Chertsey may be compared in this particular to Hyde, for instance, or to the Vale of the Cross, to Fountains, to Ripon, to Melrose, and to many others. It was in the new order of monastic development what Staines, its neighbour, had been in the old Roman order—the mark of the first stage up-river from London.

The pagan storm which all but repeated in Britain the disaster of the Saxon invasions, which all but overcame the mystic tenacity of Alfred and the positive mission of the town of Paris, swept it completely. Its abbot and its ninety monks were massacred, and it was not till late in the next century, about 950, that it arose again from its ruins. It was deliberately re-colonised again from Abingdon, and from that moment onwards it grew again into power. Donations poured upon it; one of them, not the least curious, was of land in Cardiganshire. It came from those Welsh princes who were perpetually at war with the English Crown: for religion was in those days what money is now—a thing without frontiers—and it seemed no more wonderful to the Middle Ages that an English monastery should collect its rents in an enemy's land than it seems strange to us that the modern financier should draw interest upon money lent for armament against the country of his domicile. Here also was first buried (and lay until it was removed to Windsor) the body of Henry VI.

The third of the great early foundations is Abingdon, and in a way it is the greatest, for, without direct connection with the Crown, by the mere vitality of its tradition, it became something more even than Chertsey was, wielding an immense revenue, more than half that of Westminster itself, and situated, as it was, in a small up-valley town, ruling with almost monarchical power. There could be even less doubt in the case of Abingdon than there was in the case of Chertsey that it was the creator of its own district of the Thames. It stood right in the marshy and waste spaces of the middle upper river, commanding a difficult but an important ford, and holding the gate of what was to be one of the most fruitful and famous of English vales. It can only have been from Abingdon that the culture and energy proceeded which was to build up Northern Berkshire and Oxfordshire between the Saxon and the Danish invasions. There only was established a sufficient concentration of capital for the work and of knowledge for the application of that wealth.

Like its two peers at Chertsey and at Westminster, Abingdon begins with legend. We are fairly sure of its date, 675, but the anchorite of the fifth century, "Aben," is as suspicious as the early Anglo-Saxon Chronicle itself, and still wilder are the fine and striking stories of its British origin, of its destruction under the persecution of Diocletian and of its harbouring the youth of Constantine. But the stories are at least enough to show with what violence the pomp and grandeur of the place struck the imagination of its historians.

Abingdon was, moreover, probably on account of its distance from London, more of a local centre, and, to repeat a word already used, more of a "monarchy" than the other great monasteries of the Thames Valley. This is sufficiently proved by a glance at the ecclesiastic map, such as, for instance, that published in "The Victoria History of the County of Berkshire," where one sees the manors belonging to Abingdon at the time of the Conquest all clustered together and occupying one full division of the county, that, namely, included in the great bend of the Thames which has its cusp at Witham Hill. Abingdon was the life of Northern Berkshire, and it is not fantastic to compare its religious aspect in Saxon times over against the King's towns of Wantage and Wallingford to the larger national aspect of Canterbury over against Winchester and London.

Even in its purely civic character, it acquired a position which no one of the greater northern monasteries could pretend to, through the building of its bridge in the early fifteenth century. The twin fords crossing this bend of the river were, though direct and important, difficult; when they were once bridged and the bridges joined by the long causeway which still runs across Andersey Island between the old and the new branches of the Thames, travel was easily diverted from the bridge of Wallingford to that at Abingdon, and the great western road running through Farringdon towards the Cotswolds and the valley of the Severn had Abingdon for its sort of midway market town.

These three great Benedictine monasteries form, as it were, the three nurseries or seed plots from which civilisation spread out along the Thames Valley after the destruction wrought by the first and worst barbarian invasions. All three, as we have seen, go back to the very beginning of the Christian phase of English history; the origins of all three merge in those legends which make a twilight between the fantastic stories of the earlier paganism and the clear records of the Christian epoch after the re-Latinisation of England. An outpost beyond these three is the institution of St Frideswides at Oxford. Beyond that point the upper river, gradually narrowing, losing its importance for commerce and as a highway, supported no great monastery, and felt but tardily the economic change wrought by the foundations lower down the stream.

Chertsey and Westminster certainly, and Abingdon very probably, were destroyed, or at least sacked, in the Danish invasions, but their roots lay too deep to allow them to disappear: they re-arose, and a generation before the Conquest were again by far the principal centres of production and government in the Thames Valley. Indeed, with the exception of the string of royal estates upon the banks of the river, and of the town of Oxford, Chertsey, Westminster and Abingdon were the only considerable seats of regulation and government upon the Thames, when the Conquest came to reorganise the whole of English life.

With that revolution it was evident that a great extension not only of the numbers, but especially of the organisation and power, of the monastic system would appear: that gaps left uninfluenced by it in the line of the Thames would be filled up, and all the old foundations themselves would be reconstructed and become new things.

The Conquest is in its way almost as sharp a division in the history of England as is the landing of St Augustine. In some externals it made an even greater difference to this island than did the advent of the Roman Missionaries, though of course, in the fundamental things upon which the national life is built, the re-entry of England into European civilisation in the seventh century must count as a far greater and more decisive event than its first experience of united and regular government under the Normans in the eleventh. Moreover although the Conquest largely changed the language of the island, introduced a conception of law in civil affairs with which the Anglo-Saxon aristocracy were quite unfamiliar, and began to flood England with a Gallic admixture which flowed

.uninterruptedly for three hundred years, yet it did not change the intimate philosophy of the people, and it is only the change of the intimate philosophy of a people which can have a revolutionary consequence. The Conquest found England Catholic, vaguely feudal, and, though in rather an isolated way, thoroughly European. The Normans organised that feudality, extirpated whatever was unorthodox, or slack in the machinery of the religious system, and let in the full light of European civilisation through a wide-open door, which had hitherto been half-closed.

The effect, therefore, of the Conquest was exercised upon the visible and mutable things of the country rather than upon the nourishing inward things: but it was very great, and in nothing was it greater than in its inception of new buildings and the use everywhere of stone. Under the Normans very nearly all the great religious foundations of England re-arose, and that within a generation. New houses also arose, and the mark of that time (which was a second spring throughout Europe: full of the spirit of the Crusades, and a complete regeneration of social life) was the rigour of new religious orders, and especially the transformation of the old Benedictine monotony.

Chief, of course, of these religious movements, and the pioneer of them all, was the institution of Cluny in Burgundy.

Cluny did not rise by design. It was one of those spontaneous growths which are characteristic of vigorous and creative times. Those who are acquainted with the Burgundian blood will not think it fantastic to imagine the vast reputation of Cluny to have been based upon rhetoric. It was perhaps the sonorous Burgundian facility for expression and the inheritance of oratory which belonged to Burgundian soil till Bossuet's birth, and which still belongs to it, that gave Cluny a sort of spell over the mind of Western Europe, and which made Cluny a master in the century which preceded the great change of the Crusades. From Cluny as a mother house proceeded communities instinct with the discipline and new life of the reformed order, and though it has been remarked that these communities were not numerous, in comparison to the vigour of the movement, yet it should also be noted that they were nearly always very large and wealthy, that they were in a particular and close relation to the civil government of the district in which each was planted, and that their absolute dependence upon the mother house, and their close observance of one rule, lent the whole order something of the force of an army.

The Cluniac influence came early into the Thames Valley. By the beginning of the twelfth century, and within fifty years of the Conquest, this new influence was found interpolated with and imposed upon the five centuries that had hitherto been wholly dependent upon the three great Benedictine posts. This Cluniac foundation, the first of the new houses on the Thames, was fixed upon the peninsula of Reading.

It was in 1121 that the son of the Conqueror brought the Cluniac order to the little town. From the moment of the foundation of the abbey it attracted, in part by its geographical position, in part by the fact that it was the first great new foundation upon the Thames, and in part by the accident which lent a special devotion or power to one particular house and which was in this case largely due to the discipline and character of the Cluniac order, Reading took on a very high position in England. It had about it, if one may so express oneself, something more modern, something more direct and political than was to be found in the old Benedictine houses that had preceded it. The work it had to do was less material: the fields were already drained, the life and wealth of the new civilisation had begun, and throughout the four hundred years of its existence the function of Reading was rather to entertain the Court, to assist at parliaments, and to be, throughout, the support of the monarchy. It sprang at once into this position, and its architecture symbolised to some extent the rapid command which it acquired, for it preserved to the end the characteristics of the early century in which it was erected: the Norman arch, the dog-tooth ornaments, the thick walls, the barbaric capitals of the early twelfth century.

Before the thirteenth it was in wealth equal to, and in public repute the superior of, any foundation upon the banks of the Thames with the exception of Westminster itself, and it forms, with the three Benedictine foundations, and with the later foundation of Osney, the last link in the chain of abbeys which ran unbroken from stage to stage throughout the whole length of the river. And with it ends the story of those first foundations which completed the recivilisation of the Valley.

Reading was not the only Cluniac establishment upon the Thames. Another, and earlier one, was to be found at Bermondsey; but its proximity to London and its distance down river forbid it having any place in these pages. It was founded immediately after the Conquest; Lanfranc colonised it with French monks; it became an abbacy at the very end of the fourteenth century, and was remarkable for its continual accretion of wealth, an accretion in some part due to the growing importance of London throughout its existence. At the end of the thirteenth century it stands worth £280. At the time of its dissolution, on the first of January 1538, in spite of the much higher value of money in the sixteenth century as

103

compared with the thirteenth, it stands worth over £500: £10,000 a year.

A relic of its building remained (but only a gatehouse) till 1805.

Osney also dated from the early twelfth century, and was almost contemporary with Reading.

It stood just outside the walls of Oxford Castle to the west, and upon the bank of the main stream of the Thames, and owed its foundation to the Conqueror's local governing family of Oilei. Though at the moment of its suppression it hardly counted a fifth of the revenues of Westminster (which must be our standard throughout all this examination), yet its magnificence profoundly affected contemporaries, and has left a great tradition. It must always be remembered that these great monasteries were not only receivers of revenue as are our modern rich, but were also producers or, rather, could be producers when they chose, and that therefore the actual economic power of any one foundation might always be higher, and often was very considerably higher, than the nominal revenue, the dead income, which passed to the spoliators of the sixteenth century. When a town is sacked the army gets a considerable loot, but nothing like what the value was of the city as it flourished before the siege.

At any rate, whether Osney owed its magnificence to internal industry, to a wise expenditure, or to a severity of life which left a large surplus for ornament and extension, it was for 400 years the principal building upon the upper river, catching the eye from miles away up by Eynsham meadows and forming a noble gate to the University town for those who approached it from the west by the packway, of which traces still remain, and over the bridges which the Conqueror had built. So deep was the impress of Osney upon the locality, and even upon the national Government, that Henry proposed, as in the case of Westminster, to make of the building one of his new cathedrals, and to establish there his new See of Oxford. The determination, however, lasted but for a very short time. In a few years the financial pressure was too much for him; he transferred the see to the old Church of St Frideswides, where it still remains, and gave up Osney to loot. It was looted very thoroughly.

The smaller monasteries need hardly a mention. At the head of them comes Eynsham, worth more than half as much as Osney, and a very considerable place. Founded as a colony or adjunct to Stow, in Lincolnshire, it outlived the importance of the parent house, and was at the height of its prosperity immediately before the Dissolution.

Eynsham affords a very good instance of the way in which the fabric in these superb temples disappeared. As late as the early eighteenth century there was still standing the whole of the west front; the two high towers, the splendid west window, and the sculptured doorways were complete, though they remained but as a fragment of a ruined building. A century and a half passed and the whole had disappeared, carted away to build walls and stables for the local squires, or sold by the local squires for rubble.

Of the little priory at Lechlade very little is known, save that it was founded in the thirteenth century and had disappeared long before the Reformation, while of that at Cricklade we know even less, save that it humbly survived and was counted in the "bag" at only four pounds a year.

With Dorchester, which had existed from the twelfth century, and which was worth almost half as much as Eynsham, and with the considerable Cell of Hurley which attached to Westminster, the list is complete. It is interesting to know that the church at Dorchester was saved by the local patriotism of one man, who left half his fortune for the purchase of it, and that not in order to ruin it and to sell the stones of it, but in order to preserve it: a singular man.

In a general survey of monastic influence in the Valley of the Thames, it would be natural to omit the foundations which belonged to the later Middle Ages. It was in the Dark Ages that the great Benedictine work was done, the pastures drained, the woods planted, the settlements established. It was in the early Middle Ages, in the twelfth and thirteenth centuries and in the first half of the fourteenth—in a word, before the Black Death—that the work of the new and vigorous foundations, and the revived energy of the older ones, spread Gothic architecture, scholastic learning, and the whole reinvigorated social system of the time, from Oxford to Westminster; and the historian who notes the social and economic effects of monasticism in Western Europe, however enthusiastic he may be in defence of that force, cannot with truth lend it between the Black Death and the Reformation a vigour which it did not possess. It had tended to become, in the fifteenth century, a fixed social institution like any other, one might almost say a bundle of proprietary rights like any other. And though it is easy now to perceive what ruin was caused by the sudden destruction, the contemporaries of the last age of Great Houses were perpetually considering their privilege and their immovable tradition rather than the remaining functions which the monasteries fulfilled in the State.

On this account historical notes dealing with the development of the Thames Valley would naturally omit a reference to foundations existing only from the close of the Middle Ages. But an exception must be made to this rule in the case of Sheen.

Sheen was a Charterhouse, and it merits observation not only from the peculiar characteristics of the Carthusian Order, but also from its considerable position so near to Westminster and not yet overshadowed by the greatness either of that abbey or of Chertsey. It received, from its land in England alone, a revenue of close upon two-thirds of that which Westminster enjoyed. Recent in its origin (it had existed for only just over 100 years when Henry VIII. attacked it), not without that foreign flavour which, rightly or wrongly, was ascribed in this island to the Carthusian Order, rigid in doctrine, and of a magnificent temper in the defence of religion, these Carthusians, like their brethren in London, formed a very natural target for the King's attack. I include them only because notes upon the mediæval foundations, would be quite imperfect were there no mention of Sheen, late as the origin of the community was, and little as it had to do with the historic development of the valley.

This completes the list of the greater foundations; with the lesser ones it would only be possible to deal in pages devoted to the Monastic Institution alone. The very numerous communities of friars, and the hospitals in the towns upon the Thames, cannot be mentioned, the little nunneries of Ankerwick, Burnham, and Little Marlow, the communities, early and late, of Medmenham and Cholsey, the priories of Lechlade and of Cricklade (which might have occupied a larger space than was available), must be passed over. Even Godstow, famous as it is from the early legend of Rosamond, and considerable as was its function both of education and of retreat, cannot be included in the list of those principal foundations which alone take rank as originators of the prosperity of the valley.

Several of these smaller houses went in the dissolution to swell the revenues of Bisham, the new community which Henry, as he said, intended to take the place of much that he had destroyed; and Bisham would be very well worth a considerable attention from the reader had it survived. But it did not survive. Hardly was it founded when Henry himself immediately destroyed it, and, as we shall see later, Bisham affords one of the most curious and instructive examples of the way in which that large monastic revenue, which it was certainly intended to keep in the hands of the Crown, and which, had it been so kept, would have given to England the strongest Central Government in Europe, drifted into the hands of the squires, multiplied perhaps by ten the wealth of their class, and transformed the Government of England into that oligarchy

106

which was completed in the seventeenth century, and which, though permeated and transformed by Jewish finance, is standing in a precarious strength to this day.

Westminster, Chertsey, Sheen, Reading, Abingdon, and Osney disappeared.

One writes the list straight off without considering, taking it for granted that everything which could have roused the cupidity of that generation necessarily disappeared: and as one writes it one remembers that, after all, Westminster survived. Its survival was an accident, which will be further considered. But that survival, so far from redeeming, emphasises and throws into relief the destruction of the rest.

Of these enduring monuments of human energy and, what is more important still in the control of energy, human certitude, what besides Westminster survived? Of Chertsey there is perhaps a gateway and part of a wall; of Sheen nothing; of Reading a few flints built into modern work; of Abingdon a gateway, and a buttress or two that long served to support a brewhouse; of Osney nothing, contrariwise, electric works and the slums of a modern town. All these were Westminsters. In all of these was to be discovered that patient process of production which argues the continuity, and therefore the dignity, of human civilisation. Each had the glass which we can no longer paint, the vivid, living, and happy grotesque in sculpture which only the best of us can so much as understand; each had a thousand and another thousand details of careful work in stone meant to endure, if not for ever, at least into such further centuries as might have the added faith and added knowledge to restore them in greater plenitude. The whole thing has gone. It has gone to no purpose. Nothing has been built upon it save a wandering host of rich and careworn men.

Suppose a man to have gone down the Thames when the new discussions were beginning in London and (as was customary even at the close of the Middle Ages) were spreading from town to town with a rapidity that we, who have ceased to debate ideas, can never understand. Let such a traveller or bargeman have gone down from Cricklade to the Tower, how would the Great Houses have appeared to him?

The upper river would have been much the same, but as he came to that part of it which was wealthy and populous, as he turned the corner of Witham Hill, he would already have seen far off, larger and a little nearer than the many spires of Oxford, a building such as to-day we never see save in our rare and half-deserted cathedral country towns. It was the Abbey of Osney. It would have been his landmark, as Hereford is the landmark for a

107

man to-day rowing up to Wye, or the new spire of Chichester for a man that makes harbour out of the channel past Bisham upon a rising tide. And as he passed beneath it (for, of the many branches here, the main stream took him that way) he would have seen a great and populous place with nothing ruinous in it, all well ordered, busy with men and splendid; here again that which we now look upon as a relic and a circumstance of repose was once alive and strong.

Upon his way beneath the old stone bridge which crossed the ford, and shooting between the lifted paddles of the weirs, he would, once below Oxford, have seen much the same pastures that we see to-day; but in a few hours Abingdon, the next to Osney, would have fixed his eyes as Osney had before.

Abingdon would have been to him what Noyon is on the Oise, or any of our river cathedrals in Western Europe—an apse pointing up stream, though rounded and lacking the flying buttresses of the Gothic, for it was thick, broad, and Norman. Here also, as one may believe, from its situation, trees would have shrouded somewhat what he saw. There are few such riverside apses in Christian Europe that are not screened in this manner by trees planted between the stream and them. But as he drifted farther down, before he reached the bridge, the west front would have burst upon him, quite new, exceedingly rich and proud, a strict example, one may believe, of the Perpendicular, and of what was for the first time, and for a moment only, a true English Gothic. It would have stood out before him, catching the sun of the afternoon in its maze of glass. It would have seemed a thing to endure; within his lifetime it was to be utterly destroyed.

Once more in the many reaches between Abingdon and Wallingford, the sights would have been those which a man sees now. And though at Wallingford he would have had before him a town of brilliant red tiles and timberwork, and a town perhaps larger than that which we see to-day, yet (could such a man come to life again) the contrast would not strike him here, and still less in the fields below, so much as when he came near to Reading.

That everything else of age in Reading has disappeared one need not say, but were that traveller here to-day, the thing that he would most seek for and most lack would be the bulk of the building at the farther end of the town.

One can best say what it was by saying that it was like Durham. It is true that Durham Cathedral stands upon a noble cliff overhanging a ravine, while Reading Abbey stood upon a small and irregular hill which hardly showed above the flat plains of the river meadows, but in massiveness of structure and in type of architecture Reading seems to have resembled Durham more nearly than any other of our great monuments, and to emphasise its parallelism to Durham is perhaps the best way to make the modern reader understand what we have lost.

Nothing that he had seen in this journey would more have sunk into the mind of a contemporary man, nothing that he would lack were he resuscitated to-day would leave a want more grievous. In the destruction of Reading the people of this country lost something which not even their aptitude for foreign travel can replace.

Windsor, as he passed, stood up above the right of him, not very different from what we still admire as we come down from Bray and look up to the jutting fore-tower which is worthy of Coucy. But down below Windsor (after whose bridge we to-day see nothing whatever of value), just after he had passed the wooden bridge of Staines and shot the weir of that town, the river bent southward.

The traveller would have found Pentonhook already forming or formed, and when he had got round it he would have seen soaring above him down stream the great mass of Chertsey Abbey. If Reading had the solidity and the barbaric grandeur of Durham, Chertsey had in an ecclesiastical way the vastness of Windsor, and must have seemed like a town to anyone approaching it thus down the river. The enclosed area of the abbey buildings alone covered four acres.

This impression which such a traveller would have received of the great religious houses was enhanced by something more than the magnitude and splendour of the buildings. Divided as was opinion at that moment upon their value to the State, and jealous as had become landless men of the long traditions and privileges of the monks, these still represented not only their own wealth but the general accumulation of capital and the continued prosperity of the river valley. It is true to say, in spite of the difficulty of appreciating such a truth in the light of our knowledge of what was to follow, that the destruction of such foundations would have seemed to the traveller before the Dissolution inconceivable. Nevertheless it came.

These notes are not the place in which to discuss that most difficult of all historical problems—I mean the causes which led the nation to abandon in a couple of generations the whole of its traditions and to adopt, not spontaneously but at the bidding of a comparatively small body of wealthy men, a new scheme of society. But it is of value to consider the economic aspect of the thing, and to show what it was that Henry desired to seize when his policy of Dissolution was secretly formed.

The economic function of the monastic system in the Middle

Ages, and especially in the later Middle Ages, is one to which no sufficient attention has been given by historians.

They collected, as does no modern agency, wealth from very various sources, scattered up and down the whole of the kingdom, and often farther afield, throughout Europe, and exercised the whole economic power so drawn together in one centre, and so founded a permanent nucleus of wealth in the place where the community resided.

We are indeed to-day accustomed to a similar effect in the action of our wealthy families. The rents of the London poor, a toll upon the produce of Egypt, of the Argentine, or of India, all flow into some country house in the provinces, where it revives in an effective demand for production, or lends to the whole countryside a wealth which, of itself, it could never have produced. The neighbourhood of Aylesbury, the palaces of the larger territorials, are modern examples of this truth, that the economic power of a district does not reside in its productive capacity, but in its capacity for effective demand. And it is undoubtedly true that if there were anything permanent in modern society we should be witnessing in the wealthier quarters of Paris and London, in the Riviera in the holiday part of Egypt, and in certain centres of provincial luxury in England, in France, and in Western Germany, the foundation of a permanent economic superiority.

But nothing in modern society has any roots. Where to-day is some one of these great territorial houses in fifty years there may be nothing but decay. Fashion may change from the Riviera to some other part of the Mediterranean littoral, and with fashion will go the concentration of wealth which accompanies it.

In the Middle, and especially in the latter Middle, Ages it was otherwise. The great religious houses not only tended to accumulate wealth and to perpetuate it in the same hands (they could not gamble it away nor disperse it in luxury; they could hardly waste it by mismanagement), but they were also permanently fixed on one spot.

Such an institution as Reading, for example, or as Abingdon, went on perpetually receiving its immense revenues for generation after generation, and were under no temptation or rather had no capacity for spending it elsewhere than in the situation where their actual buildings were to be found.

In this way the great monastic houses founded a tradition of local wealth which has profoundly affected the history of the Thames Valley. And if that valley is still to-day one of the chief districts wherein the economic power of England is concentrated, it owes that position mainly to the centuries during which the great foundations exercised their power upon the banks of the river.

The growth of great towns, one of the last phases of our national development, one which finds its example in the Thames Valley as elsewhere, and one to which we shall allude before closing these notes upon the river, has somewhat obscured the quality of this original accumulation of wealth along the Thames. But when we come to consider the figures of the census at an earlier time, before modern commercialism and the railway had drawn wealth and population into fewer and larger centres, we shall see how considerable was the string of towns which had grown up along the stream. And we shall especially see how fairly divided among them was the population, and, it may be presumed, the wealth and the rateable value, of the valley.

The point just mentioned in connection with the larger monastic foundations, and their artificial concentration of economic power, deserves a further elaboration, for the economic importance of a district is one of the aspects of geography which even modern analysis has dealt with very imperfectly.

Economists speak of the economic importance of such-and-such a spot because material of use to man-kind is there discovered. Thus, people commonly point to the economic importance of the valleys all round the Pennine Range in England because they contain coal and metals, and to the economic importance of a small district in South Wales for the same reason.

A further consideration has admitted that not only places where things useful to mankind are discovered, but places naturally fitted for their exchange have an economic importance peculiarly their own. Indeed, the more history is studied from the point of view of economics, the more does this kind of natural opportunity emerge, and the less does the political importance of purely productive areas appear. The mountain districts of Spain, the Cornish peninsula, were centres of metallic industry of the first importance to the Romans, but they remained poor throughout the period of Roman civilisation. To-day the farmer in the west of America, the miner and the clerk in Johannesburg, are perhaps more numerous, but as a political force no wealthier for the opportunities of their sites: the economic power which they ultimately produce is first concentrated in the centres of exchange where the wealth they produce is handled.

Now there is a third basis for the economic importance of a district, and as this third basis is indefinitely more important than the other two, it has naturally been overlooked in the analysis of the universities. This basis is the basis of residence. Given that a conqueror, or a seat of Government established by routine, is established in a particular place and chooses there to remain; or given that the pleasure attached to a particular site—its natural pleasures or the inherited grandeur of its buildings or what not— make it an established residence for those who control the expenditure of wealth, then that place will acquire an economic importance which has for its foundation nothing more material than the human will. Thither wealth, wherever produced, will flow, and there will be discovered that ultimate motive force of all production and of all exchange, the effective demand of those possessors who alone can set the industrial machine in motion.

This has been abundantly true in every period of the world's history, whenever commerce existed upon a considerable scale, or whenever a military force sufficiently universal was at the command of wealthy men.

It is particularly true to-day. To-day not the natural centres of exchange, still less the natural centres of production, determine what places in the world shall be wealthy and what shall not. The surplus of the wealth produced by the Egyptian fellaheen is carefully collected by English officials and largely consumed in Paris; the wealth produced by the manufacturers of North England is largely spent in the south of England and upon the Continent; until their recent and successful revolt, the wealth produced by the Irish peasantry was largely spent in London and upon the Riviera.

The economic importance, then, of the Thames Valley has not diminished, but increased since South England ceased to be the main field of production.

The tradition of Government, the habitual residence of the wealthy and directing classes of the community, have centred more and more in London. The old establishment of luxury in the Thames Valley has perpetually increased since the decline of its industrial and agricultural importance, and undoubtedly, if it were possible to draw a map indicating the proportion of economic demand throughout the country, the Valley of the Thames would appear, in proportion to its population, by far the most concentrated district in England, although it contains but one very large town, and although it is innocent of any very important modern industry.

It is interesting, in connection with this economic aspect of the Thames Valley, to note that, alone of the great river valleys of Europe, it has no railway system parallel to its banks. There is no series of productive centres which could give rise to such a railway system. The Great Western Railway follows the river now some distance upon one side, now some distance upon the other, as far as Oxford; but it does not depend in any way upon the stream, and

112

where the course of the stream is irregular it goes on its straight course, throwing out branch lines to the smaller towns upon the banks: for the railway depends, so far as this section is concerned, upon the industries of the Midlands and of the west. Were you to cut off the sources of carriage which it draws upon from beyond the Valley of the Thames it could not exist.

The Scheldt, the Rhine, the Rhone, the Garonne, the Seine, the Elbe, are all different in this from the Thames. The economic power of our main river valley is chiefly a spending power. It produces little and, though it exchanges more of human wealth, it is the artificial machinery of exchange rather than the physical movement of goods that enriches it.

Now this habit of residence, this settlement of the concentrated power of demand upon the banks of the Thames, was the work of the monastic houses. It may be argued that, with the commercial importance of London, and with its attainment of the position of a capital, the residence of such economic power would necessarily have spread up the Thames Valley. It is doubtful whether any such necessity as this existed. In Roman times the Thames certainly did not lead up thus in the line of wealth from London, and though it is true that water carriage greatly increased in importance after the breakdown of Roman civilisation, yet the medium by which that water carriage was utilised was the medium of the Benedictine foundations. They it was who established that continuous line of progressive agricultural development and who prepared the way for the later yet more continuous line of the full monastic effort which succeeded the Conquest.

A list of monastic institutions upon the river, if we exclude the friars, the hospitals, and such foundations as made part of town or university life, is as follows:—a priory at Cricklade, another at Lechlade, the Abbey at Eynsham (sufficiently near the stream to be regarded as riparian), the Nunnery and School of Godstow, the great Abbeys of Osney and Rewley, the Benedictine Nunnery at Littlemore, the great Abbey of Abingdon, the Abbey of Dorchester, Cholsey (but this had been destroyed before the Conquest, and was never revived), the Augustinian Nunnery at Goring, the great Cluniac Abbey at Reading, the Cell of Westminster at Hurley, the Abbey of Medmenham, the Abbey of Bisham just opposite Marlow, and the Nunnery of Little Marlow; the Nunnery of Burnham, which, though nearly a mile and a half from the stream, should count from the position of its property as a riparian foundation, the little Nunnery of Ankerwike, the great Benedictine Abbey of Chertsey, the Carthusians of Sheen, and the Benedictines of Westminster, to which may be added the foundation of Bermondsey.

113

When the end came the total number of those in control of such wide possessions was small.

Indeed it was perhaps no small cause of the unpopularity, such as it was, into which the same monasteries had locally fallen, that so much economic power was concentrated in so few hands. The greater foundations throughout the country possessed but a little more than 3000 religious, and even when all the nuns, friars, and professed religious of the towns are counted, we do not arrive at more than 8000 in religion in an England which must have had a population of at least 4,000,000, and quite possibly a much larger number; nor could the mobs foresee that the class which would seize upon the abbey lands would concentrate the means of production into still fewer hands, until at last the mass of Englishmen should have no lot in England.

Moreover, it would be an error to consider the numbers of the religious alone. The smaller foundations, and especially the convents of nuns, did certainly support but small numbers, and this probably accounts for the ease with which they were suppressed, but, on the other hand, their possessions also were small. In the case of the great foundations, though one can count but 3000 monks and canons, the number of them must be multiplied many times if we are to arrive at the total of the communities concerned. Reading, Abingdon, and the rest were little cities, with a whole population of direct dependants living within the walls, and a still larger number of families without, who indirectly depended upon the revenues of the abbey for their livelihood.

Another and perhaps a better way of presenting to a modern reader the overwhelming economic power of the mediæval monastic system, especially its economic power in the Valley of the Thames, would be to add to such a list of houses a map of that valley showing the manors in ecclesiastical hands, the freeholds and leaseholds held by the great abbeys, in addition to the livings that were within their gift; in a word, a map giving all their different forms of revenue.

Such a map would show the Valley of the Thames and its tributaries covered with ecclesiastical influence upon every side.

Even if we confined ourselves to the parishes upon the actual banks of the river, the map would present a continuous stretch of possessions upon either side from far above Eynsham down to below bridges.

The research that would be necessary for the establishment of such a complete list would require a leisure which is not at the disposal of the present writer, but it is possible to give some conception of what the monastic holdings were by drawing up a list confined to but a small part of these holdings and showing therefore a fortiori what the total must have been.

In this list I concern myself only with the eight largest houses in the whole length of the river. I do not mention parishes from which the revenues were not important (though these were numerous, for the abbeys held a large number of small parcels of land). I do not mention the very numerous holdings close to the river but not actually upon it (such as Burnham or Watereaton), nor, which is most important of all, do I count even in the riparian holdings such foundations as were not themselves set upon the banks of the Thames. Whatever Thames land paid rent to a monastery not actually situated upon the banks of the river, I omit. Finally the list, curtailed as it is by all these limitations, concerns only the land held at the moment of the Dissolution. Scores of holdings, such as those of Lechlade, which was dissolved in Catholic times, Windsor, which was exchanged as we have seen at the time of the Conquest, I omit and confine myself only to the lands held at the time of the Dissolution.

Yet these lands—though they concern only eight monasteries, though I mention only those actually upon the banks of the river, and though I omit from the list all small payments—put before one a series of names which, to those familiar with the Thames, seems almost like a voyage along the stream and appears to cover every portion of the landscape with which travellers upon the river are familiar. Thus we have Shifford, Eynsham, South Stoke, Radley, Cumnor, Witham, Botley, the Hinkseys, Sandford, Shillingford, Swinford, Medmenham, Appleford, Sutton, Wittenham, Culham, Abingdon, Goring, Cowley, Littlemore, Cholsey, Nuneham, Wallingford, Pangbourne, Streatley, Stanton Harcourt; and all this crowd of names upon the upper river is arrived at without counting such properties as attached to the great monasteries within towns, as, for example, to the monasteries of Oxford. It is true that not all these names represent complete manorial ownership. In a number of cases they stand for portions of the manor only, but even in this list ten at least, and possibly twelve, stand for complete manorial ownership. Then one must add Sonning, Wargreave, Tilehurst, Chertsey, Egham, Cobham, Richmond, Ham, Mortlake, Sheen, Kew, Chiswick, Staines, etc., of which many of the most important, such as Staines, are full manorial possessions.

It is clearly evident, from such a very imperfect and rapidly drawn list, what was the economic power of the great houses, and one may conclude, even from the basis of such imperfect evidence, that the directing force of economic effort throughout the Thames Valley was to be found, right up to the Dissolution, in the chapter

115

houses of Reading, of Chertsey, and of Westminster, of Abingdon and of the lesser houses.

In a word, the business of Henry might be compared to what may be in future the business of some democratic European Government when it lays its hands upon the fortunes of the great financial houses, but with this double difference, that the confiscation to which Henry bent himself was a confiscation of capital whose product did not leave the country, and could not be used for anti-national purposes, as also that it was the confiscation of wealth which never acted secretly and which had no interest, as have our chief moneylenders, in political corruption. It was a vast undertaking and, in the truest sense of the word, a revolutionary one, such as Europe had not seen until that moment, and perhaps has not seen since.

It was effected with ease, because there did not reside in the public opinion of the time any strong body of resistance.

The change of religion, in so far as a change was threatened (and upon that the mass of the parish priests themselves, and still more the mass of the laity, were very hazy), did not affect the mind of a people famous throughout Europe for their intense and often superstitious devotion; but in some odd way the segregation of the great communities, their vast wealth, and perhaps an external contradiction between their original office and their present privilege, forbade any united or widespread enthusiasm in their defence.

Englishmen rose upon every side when they thought that the vital mysteries of the Faith were threatened. The risings were only put down by the use of foreign mercenaries and by the most execrable cruelty, nor would even these means have sufficed had the rebels formed a clear plan, or had the purpose of Henry himself in matters of religion been definite and capable of definite attack. But the country, though ready to fight for Dogma, was not ready to fight for the monasteries. It might, perhaps, have fought if the attack upon them had been direct and universal. If Henry had laid down a programme of suppressing religious bodies in general, he probably could not have carried it out, but he laid down no such programme. The Dissolution of the smaller houses was imagined by the most devout to be a statesmanlike measure. Many of them, like Medmenham, were decayed; their wealth was not to be used for the private luxury of the King or of nobles; it was to swell the revenues of the greater foundations or to be applied to pious or honourable public use. But the example once given, the attack upon the greater houses necessarily followed; and the whole episode is a vivid lesson in the capital principle of statesmanship that men are governed by

116

routine and by the example of familiar things. Render possible to the mass of men the conception that the road, they habitually follow is not a necessity of their lives, and you may exact of them almost any sacrifice or hope to see them witness without disgust almost any enormity.

Moreover, the great monasteries were each severally tricked. The one was asked to surrender at one time, another at another; the one for this reason, the other for that. The suppression of Chertsey, the example perpetually recurring in these pages, was solemnly promised to be but a transference of the community from one spot to another; then when the transference had taken place the second community was ruthlessly destroyed. There is ample evidence to show that each community had its special hope of survival, and that each, until quite the end of the process, regarded its fate, when that fate fell upon it, as something exceptional and peculiar to itself. Some, or rather many, purchased temporary exemption, doubtless secure in the belief that their bribe would make that extension permanent. Their payments were accepted, but the contracts depending upon them were never fulfilled.

When the Dissolution had taken place, apart from the private loot, which was enormous, and to which we shall turn a few pages hence, a methodical destruction took place on the part of the Crown.

In none of the careless waste which marked the time is there a worse example than in the case of Reading. The lead had already been stripped from the roof and melted into pigs; the timbers of the roof had already been rotting for nearly thirty years, when Elizabeth gave leave for such of them as were sound to be removed. Some were used in the repairing of a local church; a little later further leave was given for 200 cartloads of freestone to be removed from the ruins. But they showed an astonishing tenacity. The abbey was still a habitation before the Civil Wars, and even at the end of the eighteenth century a very considerable stretch of the old walls remained.

Westminster was saved. The salvation of Westminster is the more remarkable in that the house was extremely wealthy.

Upon nothing has more ink been wasted in the minute research of modern history than upon an attempted exact comparison between modern and mediæval economics.

It is a misfortune that those who are best fitted to appreciate the economic problems and science of the modern world are, either by race or religion, or both, cut off from the mediæval system, and even when they are acquainted with the skeleton, as it were, of that body of Christian Europe, are none the less out of sympathy with, or even ignorant of, its living form and spirit.

117

The particular department of that inquiry which concerns anyone who touches the vast economic revolution produced by the Dissolution of the monasteries is the comparison of values (as measured in the precious metals) between the early sixteenth century and the early twentieth.

No sensible man needs to be told that such a comparison is one of the very numerous parts of historical inquiry in which a better result is arrived at in proportion as the matter is more generally and largely observed. It is one in which detail is more fatal to a man even than inaccuracy, and it is one in which hardly a single observer who has been really soaked in his subject has avoided the most ludicrous conclusions.

Again, no man of common sense need be told that a rigid multiple is absolutely impossible of discovery. The search for such a multiple is like a search for an index number which shall apply to all the varying economic habits of the modern world. One cannot say: "Multiply prices by 10" or "Multiply prices by 20," and thus afford the modern reader a sound basis; but one can say, after some observation: "Multiply by such-and-such a multiple" (wherever very large and varied expenditure is concerned) and you will certainly have a minimum; though how much more such expenditure may have represented in those very different and far simpler social circumstances cannot be precisely determined. What, then, is the rough multiple that will give us our minimum?

The inquiry has been prosecuted by more than one authority upon the basis of wheat. One may say that wheat in normal years in the early sixteenth century stood at about an eighth of wheat in what I may call the normal years of the nineteenth, before the influx of Colonial produce began to be serious, and before the depreciation of silver combined with other causes to disturb prices.

Those who have taken wheat for their basis, recognising, as even they must do, that 8 is far too low a multiple, are willing to grant 10, and sometimes even 12, and this way of calculating, largely because it is a ready rule, has entered into many books upon the Reformation. The early Tudor penny is turned into the modern shilling.

But this basis of calculation is false, because the eating of wheaten bread was not then the universal thing it is to-day. The English proletarian of to-day is, in comparison with the large well-to-do class of his fellow-citizens, a far poorer man than his ancestry ever were. Wheaten bread is, indeed, his necessity, but good fresh meat (for example) is an exception for him.

Now the Englishmen of earlier times made beef a necessity, and yet we find that beef will permit a higher multiple than wheat.

118

Beef will give you a multiple of 12, and just as wheat, giving you a multiple of 8, permits a somewhat higher general multiple, so beef, giving you a multiple of 12, permits a higher one. So if we were to make beef our staple instead of wheat we should get a multiple of 13 or 14 by which to turn the money of the first third of the sixteenth century into the money of our own time.

But beef, in its turn, is not a fair standard; during much of the year pork had, under the circumstances of the time, to be eaten instead of fresh meat. Pork is to-day almost the only meat all the year round of many labourers on the land. Now pork gives a still higher multiple: it gives 20. For the pound that you would now give in Chichester Market for a breeding sow, you gave in the early years of the sixteenth century a shilling. So here you have another article of common consumption which gives you a multiple of 20.

Strong ale gives you a higher multiple still—one of nearly 24. You could then get strong ale at a penny a gallon. You will hardly get it at two shillings a gallon to-day; and yet it is made of the same materials. The small ale of the hayfield will give you almost any multiple you like; it is from eightpence to ninepence a gallon now: it was often given away in the sixteenth century as water would be.

The consideration of but a few sets of prices such as those we have quoted shows that the ordinary multiple might be anything between 8 and 24, with a prejudice in favour of the higher rather than the lower figure. But there are other lines of proof which converge upon the matter, and which permit a greater degree of certitude. For instance, even after the rise in prices in the early part of Elizabeth's reign, while sixpence a week is thought low for the board and lodging of a working man, a shilling is thought very high, and is only given in the case of first-rate artisans; and if we consider the pre-Reformation period, when the position of the labourer was, of course, much better than it was under Elizabeth, or ever has been since, we find something of the same scale. A penny a day is thought a rather mean allowance, but twopence a day is a first-rate extra board wage.

Again, in Henry VIII.'s first poll tax it is taken for granted that many labourers have less than a pound a year in actual wages, and that wages over this sum, up to two pounds, for instance, form a sort of aristocracy of labour that can afford to pay taxation. Of course some part of the wages so counted were paid in part board and lodging, especially in the agricultural industries, but still, the reception of 240 pence for a year's work in money gives you a multiple of far more than 20: you will not get a man about a house and garden for less than thirty pounds though you feed and house him, and the unhoused outside labourer gets, first and last, over fifty pounds at the least.

When the Reformation was in full swing the currency was debased almost out of recognition, and before the death of Edward VI. prices are rendered so fictitious by inflation that they are useless for our purpose. It is only with the currency of Elizabeth that they became true measures of value once more.

It is useless, therefore, to follow the inquiry after the Dissolution of the monasteries, for not only was the currency at sixes and sevens, but true prices were also rapidly rising with the influx of precious metals from Spain and America.

I have said enough in this very elementary sketch to show that a general multiple of 20, when one considers wages as well as staple foods, is as high as can be fixed safely, while a general multiple of 12 is certainly too low.

But even to multiply by 20 is by no means enough if one is to appreciate the social meaning of such-and-such a large income in the first part of Henry VIII.'s reign.

A brief historical essay, such as is this, is no place in which to discuss any general theory of economics; were there space to do so, even in an elementary fashion, it would be possible to show how the increase of wealth in a state is, on account of the increased elasticity in circulation of the currency, almost independent of the movement of prices. But without going into formulæ; of this complexity, a couple of homely comparisons will suffice to show what a much larger thing a given income was in the early sixteenth century, than its corresponding amount in values is to-day.

Consider a man with some £2000 a year travelling through modern Europe. Prices, in the competition of modern commerce and the ease of modern travel, are levelled up very evenly throughout the area that he traverses. Yet such a man, should he settle in a village of Spanish peasants, would appear of almost illimitable wealth, because he would have at his command an almost indefinite amount of those simple necessities which form the whole category of their consumable values. Or again, let such a man settle in a place where the variety of consumable values is large, but where the distribution of wealth is fairly equal, and the small income, therefore, a normal social phenomenon—as, for instance, among the lower middle class of Paris-there again his £2000 a year would be of much greater effect than in a society where wealth was unequally divided, for it would produce that effect in a medium where the satisfaction of nearly every individual around him was easily reached upon perhaps a tenth of such an income.

When all this is taken into consideration we can begin to see what the great monasteries were at the time of their dissolution. It is hardly an exaggeration to multiply the list of mere values by 20 to bring it into the terms of modern currency. A place worth close on £2000 a year (as was, for instance, Ramsey Abbey) meant an income of not far short of £40,000 a year in our money, to go by prices alone. And that £40,000 a year was spent in an England in which nine-tenths of the luxury of our modern rich was unknown, in which the squire was usually but three or four times richer than one of his farmers, in which great wealth, where it existed, attached rather to an office than to a person. In general, the multiple of 20 must be further multiplied by a coefficient which is not arithmetically determinable, but which we see I to be very large by a general comparison of the small, poor, and equable society of the early sixteenth century with the complex, huge, wealthy, and wholly iniquitous society of our own day.

Supposing, for instance, we take the high multiple of 20, and say that the revenues of Westminster at its dissolution in the first days of 1540 were some £80,000 a year in our modern money, we are far underestimating the economic position of Westminster in the State. There are to-day many private men in London who dispose of as great an income, and who, for all their ostentation, are not remarkable; but the income of Westminster in the early sixteenth century, when wealth was far more equally divided than it is now, and when the accumulation of it was far less, was a very different matter to what we mean to-day by £80,000 a year. It produced more of the effect which we might to-day imagine would be produced by a million. The fortune of but very few families could so much as compare with it, and the fortunes of individual families, especially of wealthy families, were, during the existence of a strong king, highly perilous, and often cut short; nothing could pretend to equal such an economic power but the Crown, which then was, and which remained until the victory of the aristocracy in the Civil Wars, by far the richest legal personality in Britain. The temptation to sack Westminster was something like the temptation presented to our financial powers to-day to get at the rubber of the Congo Basin or at the unexploited coal of Northern China.

By a miracle that temptation was withstood. For the moment Henry intended to construct a bishopric with its cathedral out of the old corporation and abbey. He might have done so and yet have yielded immediately after to his cupidity, as he did with the Cathedral of Osney. It ended in the form which it at present maintains. The greater part of its revenues were, of course, stolen, but the fabric was spared and enough income was retained to permit the continuous life of Westminster to our own time.

Men are slow to conceive what might have been—nay, what almost was—in their national history; it seems difficult to our generation to imagine Westminster Abbey absent only from the national life; yet Abingdon is gone, all but a gateway, Reading all but a few ruined walls, Chertsey has utterly disappeared, so has Osney, so has Sheen—to mention the great river houses alone: Westminster alone survives, and the only reason it survives is that it had about it at the time of the destruction of the monasteries a royal flavour, and that its existence helped to bolster up the Tudors. But for that it would have been sold like the rest, the lead would have been stripped from its roof, the glass broken and thrown aside, and a Cecil or a Howard would have built himself a palace with the stones. It is but a chance that the words "Westminster Abbey" mean more to us to-day than "Woburn Abbey," "Bewley Abbey" or any one of the scores of "Abbeys," "Priories," and the rest, which are the names of our country houses.

Chertsey and Abingdon were less fortunate than Westminster.

Chertsey, indeed, has so thoroughly disappeared that it might be taken as a symbol of all that England had been for the thirty generations since Christianity had come to her, and then, in two generations of men, ceased suddenly to be. There is, perhaps, not one in a thousand of the vague Colonials who regard Westminster Abbey as a sort of inevitable centre for Britishers and Anglo-Saxons, who has so much as heard of Chertsey. There is perhaps but one in a hundred of historical students who could attach a definite connection to the name, and yet Chertsey came next in the list of the great Benedictine Abbeys; Chertsey also was coeval with England.

Chertsey went the way of them all. The last abbot, John Cordery, surrendered it in the July of 1537, but he and his community were not immediately dispersed, they were taken off to fill that strange new foundation of Bisham, of which we shall hear later in connection with the river, and which in its turn immediately disappeared. Not a year had passed, the June of 1538 was not over, when the new community at Bisham was scattered as the old one at Chertsey had been.

Of the abbey itself nothing is left but a broken piece of gateway, and the few stones of a wall. But a relic of it remains in Black Cherry Fair, a market granted to the abbey in the fifteenth century and formerly held upon St. Anne's Hill and upon St. Anne's Day.

The fate of this monastery has something about it particularly tragic, for the abbot and the monks of Chertsey when they surrendered did so in the full expectation of continuing their monastic life at Bisham, and if Bisham was treacherously destroyed immediately after the fault does not lie at their door.

With Abingdon it was otherwise. The last prior was perhaps the least steadfast of all the many bewildered or avaricious characters that meet us in the story of the Dissolution. He was one Thomas Rowland, who had watched every movement of Henry's mind, and had, if possible, gone before. He did not even wait until the demand was made to him, but suggested the abandonment of the trust which so many generations of Englishmen had left in his hands, and he had a reward in the gift not only of a very large pension but also of the Manor of Cumnor, which had been before the destruction of the religious orders the sanatorium or country house of the monks. He obtained it: and from his time on Cumnor has borne an air of desolation and of murder, nor does any part of his own palace remain.

When any organised economic system disappears, there is nothing more interesting in history than to watch the process of its replacement: for example, the gradual disappearance of pagan slavery, and its replacement by the self-governing peasantry of the Middle Ages, with all the consequence of that change, affords some of the best reading in Continental records. But the Dissolution of the English monasteries has this added interest, that it was an immediate, and therefore an overwhelming, change; there was hardly a warning, there was no delay. Suddenly, not within the lifetime of a man, but within that of a Parliament, from one year to another, a good quarter of the whole economic power of the nation was utterly transformed. Nothing like it has been known in European history.

What filled the void so made? The answer to this question is, the Oligarchy: the landed class which had been threatening for so long to assume the Government of England stepped into the shoes of the great houses, and by this addition to their already considerable power achieved the destruction of the monarchy and within 100 years proceeded to the ordering of the English people under a small group of wealthy men, a form of Government which to this day England alone of all Christian nations suffers or enjoys.

This general statement must not be taken to mean that the oligarchic system, whose basis lies in the ownership of land, was immediately created by the Dissolution of the great monasteries. The development of the territorial system of England, of which system the banks of the Thames afford as good a picture as any in England, can be traced certainly from Saxon, and conjecturally from Roman, times.

The Roman estate was, presumably, the direct ancestor of the manor, and the Saxon thegns were perhaps most of them in blood, and nearly all of them in social constitution, descended from the owners of the Roman Villas which had seen the petty but recurrent pirate invasions of the fifth and sixth centuries.

But though the manorial arrangement, with its village lords and their dependent serfs, was common to the whole of the West, and could be found on the Rhine, in Gaul, and even in Italy, in Saxon England it had this peculiarity, that there was no systematic organisation by which the local land-owner definitely recognised a feudal superior, and through him the power of a Central Government. Or rather, though in theory such recognition had grown up towards the end of the Saxon period, in practice it hardly existed, and when William landed the whole system of tenure was in disorder, in the sense that the local lord of the village was not accustomed to the interference of a superior, and that no groups of lords had come into existence by which the territorial system could be bound in sheaves, as it were, and the whole of it attached to one central point at the royal Court.

Such a system of groups had arisen in Gaul, and to that difference ultimately we owe the French territorial system of the present day, but William the Norman's new subjects had no comprehension of it.

It was upon this account that even those manors which he handed over to his French kindred and dependants were scattered, and that, though he framed a vigorous feudal rule centring in his own hands, the ancient customs of the populace, coupled with the lack of any bond between scattered and locally independent units, forbade that rule to endure.

William's order was not a century old when the recrudescence of the former manorial independence was felt in the reign of Henry II. Under the personal unpopularity of his son, John, it blazed out into successful revolt, and, in spite of the veil thrown over underlying and permanent customs by such strong feudal kings as the first and the third Edwards, the independence and power of the village landlord remained the chief and growing character of English life. It expressed itself in the quality of the local English Parliament, in the support of the usurping Lancastrian dynasty—in twenty ways that converge and mingle towards the close of the Middle Ages.

But after the Dissolution of the monasteries this power of the squires takes on quite a different complexion: the land-owning class, from a foundation for the National Government, became, within two generations of the Dissolution, the master of that Government.

For many centuries previous to the sixteenth the old funded wealth of the Crown had been gradually wasting, at the expense of the Central National Government and to the profit of the squires. But the alienation was never complete. There are plenty of cases in which the Crown is found resuming the proprietorship of a manor to which it had never abandoned the theoretical title. With the Tudors such cases become rarer and rarer, with the Stuarts they cease.

The cause of this rapid enfeeblement of the Crown lay largely in the changed proportion of wealth. The King, until the middle of the sixteenth century, had been far wealthier than any one of his subjects. By a deliberate act, the breaking up of ecclesiastical tenure, the Crown offered an opportunity to the wealthier of those subjects so enormously to increase their revenues as to overshadow itself; in a little more than a century after the throwing open of the monastic lands the King is an embarrassed individual, with every issue of expenditure ear-marked, every source of it controlled, and his very person, as it were, mortgaged to a plutocracy. The squires had not only added to their revenues the actual amounts produced by the sites and estates of the old religious foundations, they had been able by this sudden accession of wealth to shoot ahead in their competition with their fellow-citizens. The counterweight to the power of the local landlord disappeared with the disappearance of the monastery.

To show how the religious houses had furnished a powerful counterweight by which the Central Government and the populace could continue to oppose the growing power of the landed oligarchy, we may take all the southern bank of the Thames from Buscot to Windsor. We find at the time of the Conquest twelve royal manors and fifteen religious; only the nine remaining were under private lords. Four and a half centuries later, at the time of the Dissolution, the royal manors have passed for the most part into private hands, but the manors in the hands of the religious houses have actually increased in number.

At this point it is important to note an economic phenomenon which appears at first sight accidental, but which, on examination, is found to spring from calculable political causes. At the moment of the Dissolution it was apparently in the power of the Crown to have concentrated the revenues of all these monastic manors into its own hands, and this typical stretch of country, the Berkshire shore, shows how economically powerful the Central Government of England might have become had the property surrendered to the Crown been kept in the hands of the King.

The modern reader will be tempted to inquire why it was not so kept.

Most certainly Henry intended to keep, if not the whole of it (for he must reward his servants, and he was accustomed to do things largely), yet at least the bulk of it in the Royal Treasury, and had he been able to do so the Central Government of England would have become by far the strongest thing in Europe. It is conceivable, though in consideration of the national character doubtful, that with so powerful an instrument of government, England, instead of standing aside from the rapid bureaucratic recasting of European civilisation which was the work of the French Crown, might have led the way in that chief of modern experiments. One can imagine the Stuarts, had they possessed revenue, doing what the Bourbons did: one can imagine the modern State developing under an English Crown wealthier than any other European Government, and the rebirth of Europe happening just to the north, instead of just to the south, of the Channel.

But the speculation is vain. As a fact, the whole of the new wealth slipped rapidly from between the fingers of the English King.

When of three forces which still form an equilibrium two are stationary and one is pressing upon these two, then, if either of the stationary forces be removed, that which was pressing upon both overwhelms the stationary force that remains. The monastic system had been marking time for over 100 years, and in certain political aspects of its power had perhaps slightly dwindled. The monarchy, for all its splendour, was in actual resources no more than it had been for some generations. Pressing upon either of these two institutions was the rising and still rising force of the squires. It is not wonderful that under such conditions the spoil fell to the younger and advancing power.

Consider, for example, the extraordinary anxiety of so apparently powerful a king as Henry for the formal consent of the Commons to his acts. It has been represented as part of the Tudor national policy and what not, but those who write thus have not perhaps smiled, as has the present writer, over the names of those who sat for the English shires in the Parliament which assented to the Dissolution of the great monastic houses. Here is a Ratcliffe from Northumberland, and a Collingwood; here is a Dacre, a Musgrave, a Blenkinsop; the Constables are there, and the Nevilles from Yorkshire; the Tailboys of Lincoln, a Schaverell, a Throgmorton, a Ferrers, a Gascoyne; and of course, inevitably, sitting for Bedfordshire, a hungry Russell.

Here is a Townshend, a Wingfield, a Wentworth, an Audley— all from East Anglia—a Butler; from Surrey a Carew, and that

FitzWilliam whose appetite for the religious spoils proved so insatiable; here is a Blount out of Shropshire; a Lyttleton, a Talbot (and yet another Russell!), a Darrell, a Paulet, a Courtney, (to see what could be picked up in his native county of Devon), and after him a Grenfell. These are a few names taken at random to show what humble sort of "Commons" it was that Henry had to consider. They are significant names; and the "Constitution" had little to do then, and has little to do now, with their domination. Wealth was and is their instrument of power.

That such men could ultimately force the Government is evident, but what is remarkable, perhaps, is the extraordinary rapidity with which the Crown was stripped of its new wealth by the gentry, and this can only be explained in two ways:

First, there was the rapid change in prices which rose from the Spanish importation of precious metals from America, the effect of which was now reaching England; and, secondly, the Tudor character.

As to the first, it put the National Government, dependent as it still largely was upon the customary and fixed payments, into a perpetual embarrassment. Where it still received nothing but the customary shilling, it had to pay out three for material and wages, whose price had risen and was rising. In this embarrassment, in spite of every subterfuge and shift, the Crown was in perpetual, urgent, and increasing need. Rigid and novel taxes were imposed, loans were raised and not repaid, but something far more was needed to save the situation, with prices still rising as the years advanced. Ready money from those already in possession of perhaps half the arable land of England was an obvious source, and into their pockets flowed, as by the force of gravitation, the funded wealth which had once supported the old religion. Hardly ever at more than ten years' purchase, sometimes at far less, the Crown turned its new rentals into ready money, and spent that capital as though it had been income.

The Tudor character was a second cause.

It is a pleasing speculation to conceive that, if some character other than a Tudor had been upon the throne, not all at least of this national inheritance would have been dissipated. One can imagine a character—tenacious, pure, narrow and subtle, intent upon dignity, and with a natural suspicion of rivals—which might have saved some part of the estates for posterity. Charles I., for example, had he been born 100 years earlier, might very well have done the thing.

But the Tudors, for all their violence, were fundamentally weak. There was always some vice or passion to interrupt the continuity of their policy—even Mary, who was not the offspring of caprice, had inherited the mental taint of the Spanish house—and before the last of the family had died, while still old men were living who, as children, had seen the monasteries, nearly all this vast treasure had found its way into the pockets of the squires. In the middle of the seventeenth century every one of these villages is under a private landlord: before the close of it even the theoretical link of their feudal dependence upon the Crown is snapped: and the two centuries between that time and our own have seen the power of the new landlords steadily maintained and latterly vastly increased.

Apart from the transfer of the monastic manors there was yet another way in which the Dissolution of the religious houses helped on the establishment of the landed oligarchy in the place of the old National Government. The monasteries had owned not only these full manorial rights, but also numerous parcels of land scattered up and down in manors whose lordship was already in private hands. These parcels, like the small lay freeholds, which they resembled, formed nuclei of resistance to the increasing power of the squires.

The point is of very considerable importance, though not easy to seize for anyone unacquainted with the way in which the territorial oligarchy has been built up or ignorant of the present conditions of English village life.

At the close of the Middle Ages the lord of a manor in England, though possessed of a larger proportion of the land than were his colleagues in other countries, but rarely could claim so much as one half of the acreage of a parish; the rest was common, in which his rights were strictly limited and defined, to the advantage of the poor, and also side by side with common was to be found a number of partially and wholly independent tenures, over which the squire had little or no control, from copyholds which did furnish him occasional sums of money, to freeholds which were practically independent of him.

The monasteries possessed parcels of this sort everywhere. To give but one example: Chertsey had twenty acres of freehold pasturage in the Manor of Cobham; but it is useless to give examples of a thing which was as common as the renting of a house to-day. Now these small parcels formed a most valuable foundation upon which the independence of similar lay parcels could repose. The squire might be tempted to bully a four-acre man out of his land, but he could not bully the Abbot of Abingdon, or of Reading. And so long as these small parcels were sanctioned by the power of the great houses, so long they were certain to endure in the hands even of the smallest and the humblest of the tenants. To-day in a modern village where a gentleman possesses such an island of land, better still where several do, there at once arises a tendency and an opportunity for the smaller men to acquire and to retain. The present writer could quote a Sussex village in the centre of which were to be found, but thirty years ago, more than half-a-dozen freeholds. They disappeared: in its prosperity "The Estate" extinguished them. The next heir in his embarrassment has handed over the whole lump to a Levantine for a loan. Had the Old Squire spared the small freeholds they would have come in as purchasers and would have increased their number during the later years when the principal landlord, his son, was gradually falling into poverty and drink.

When the monasteries were gone the disappearance of the small men gradually began. It was hastened by the extinction of that old tradition which made the Church a customary landlord exacting quit rents always less than the economic value of the land, and, what with the security of tenure and the low rental, creating a large tenant right. This tenant right vested in the lucky dependants of the Church did indeed create intense local jealousies that help to account for much of the antagonism to the monastic houses. But the future showed that the benefits conferred, though irregular and privileged, were more than the landless men could hope to expect when they had exchanged the monk for the squire.

Finally, the Dissolution of the religious houses strengthened the squires in the mere machinery of the constitution. Before that Dissolution the House of Lords was a clerical house. Had you entered the Council of Henry VII. when Parliament sat at Westminster you would have seen a crowd of mitres and of croziers, bishops and abbots of the great abbeys, among whom, here and there, were some thirty lay lords. This clerical House of Lords, sprung largely from the populace, possessed only of life tenure, was a very different thing from the House of Lords that succeeded the Dissolution. That immediately became a committee, as it were, of the landed class; and a committee of the landed class the House of Lords remained until quite the last few years, when the practice of purchase has admitted to it brewers, money-lenders, Colonial speculators, and, indeed, anyone who can furnish the sum required by a woman or a secret party fund. A concrete example is often of value in the illustration of a general process, and at the expense of a digression I propose to lay before the reader as excellent a picture as we have of the way in which the Dissolution of the monasteries not only emphasised the position of the existing territorial class, but began to recruit it with elements drawn from every quarter, and, while it established the squires in power, taught them to be careless of the origin or of the end of the families admitted to their rank.

For this purpose I can find no better example than that of the family of Williams, which by the licence of custom we have come to call "Cromwell"; the most famous member of this family stands out in English history as the typical squire who led the Forces of his Order against the impoverished Monarchy, and so reduced that emblem of Government to the simulacrum which it still remains.

Putney, by Thames-side, was the home of their very lowly beginnings.

Of the descent of the Williams throughout the Middle Ages nothing is known. Much later they claimed relationship with certain heads of the Welsh clans, but the derivation is fantastic. At any rate a certain Williams was keeping a public-house in Putney in the generation which saw the first of the Reformers. His name was Morgan, and the "Ap William" or "Williams" which he added to that name was an affix due to the Welsh custom of calling a man by his father's name; for surnames had not yet become a rule in the Principality. He may have come, and probably did, from Glamorganshire, and that is all we can say about him; though we must admit some weight in Leland's contemporary evidence that his son, Richard, was born in the same county, at a place called Llanishen. Anyhow, there he is, keeping his public-house in the first years of the sixteenth century by the riverside at Putney.

There lived in the same hamlet (which was a dependency of the manor of Wimbledon) a certain Cromwell or Crumwell, who was also called Smith; but this obscure personage should most probably be known by the first of these two names, for his humble business was the shoeing of horses, and the second appellation was very probably a nickname arising from that trade. He also added beer-selling to his other work, and this common occupation may have formed a link between him and his neighbour, Morgan ap William.

The next stage in the story is not perfectly clear. Smith or Crumwell had a son and two daughters, the son was called Thomas, and the daughter that concerns us was called Katherine. It is highly probable, according to modern research into the records of the manor, that Morgan ap William married Katherine. But the matter is still in some doubt. There are not a few authorities, some of them painstaking, though all of them old, who will have it that the blacksmith's son, Thomas, loved Morgan ap William's sister, instead of its being the other way about. It is not easy to establish the exact relationship between two public-house keepers who lived as neighbours in a dirty little village 400 years ago.

Thomas proceeded to an astonishing career; he left his father's forge, wandered to Italy, may have been present at the sack of Rome, and was at last established as a merchant in the city of

130

London. When one says "merchant" one is talking kindly. His principal business then, as throughout his life, was that of a usurer, and he showed throughout his incredible adventures something of that mixture of simplicity and greed, with a strange fixity in the oddest of personal friendships, which amuses us to-day in our company promoters and African adventurers. His abilities recommended him to Wolsey, and when that great genius fell, Cromwell was, as the most familiar of historical traditions represents him, faithful to his master.

Whether this faithfulness recommended him to the King or not, it is difficult to say. Probably it did, for there is nothing that a careful plotter will more narrowly watch in an agent than his record of fidelity in the past.

Henry fixed upon him to be his chief instrument in the suppression of the monasteries. His lack of all fixed principle, his unusual power of application to a particular task, his devotion to whatever orders he chose to obey, and his quite egregious avarice, all fitted him for the work his master ordered.

How the witty scoundrel accomplished that business is a matter of common history. Had he never existed the monasteries would have fallen just the same, perhaps in the same manner, and probably with the same despatch. But fate has chosen to associate this revolution with his name—and to his presence in that piece of confiscation we owe the presence in English history of the great Oliver; for Oliver, as will be presently seen, and all his tribe were fed upon no other food than the possessions of the Church. Cromwell, in his business of suppressing the great houses, embezzled quite cynically—if we can fairly call that "embezzlement" which was probably countenanced by the King, to whom account was due. Indeed, it is plainly evident from the whole story of that vast economic catastrophe which so completely separates the England we know from the England of a thousand years—the England of Alfred, of Edward I., of Chaucer, and of the French Wars—it is evident from the whole story, that the flood of confiscated wealth which poured into the hands of the King's agents and squires was a torrent almost impossible to control; Henry VIII. was glad enough to be able to retain, even for a year or two, one half of the spoils.

We know, for instance, that the family of Howard (which was then already of more than a century's standing) took everything they could lay their hands on in the particular case of Bridlington—pyxes, chalices, crucifixes, patens, reliquaries, vestments, shrines, every saleable or meltable thing, and the cattle and pigs into the bargain, and never dreamt of giving account to the King.

With Cromwell, the embezzlement was more systematic: it

131

was a method of keeping accounts. But our interest lies in the fact that the process was accompanied by that curious fidelity to all with whom he was personally connected, which forms so interesting a feature in the sardonic character of this adventurer. It is here that we touch again upon the family of Morgan ap William, the public-house keeper of Putney.

When Cromwell was at the height of his power he lifted out from the obscurity of his native kennel a certain Richard Williams, calling him now "cousin" and now "nephew." We may take it that the boy was a nephew, and that the word "cousin" was used only in the sense of general relationship which attached to it at that time. If Cromwell had been a man of a trifle more distinction, or of tolerable honesty, we might even be certain that this young fellow was the legitimate son of his sister Katherine, and, indeed, it is much the more probable conclusion at which we should arrive to-day. But Cromwell himself obscured the matter by alluding to his relative as "Williams (alias Cromwell)," and there must necessarily remain a suspicion as to the birth and real status of his dependant.

In 1538 this young Richard Williams got two foundations handed over to him—both in Huntingdon, and together amounting in value to about £500 a year.

We have seen on an earlier page how extremely difficult or impossible it is to estimate exactly in modern money the figures of the Dissolution. We have agreed that to multiply by twenty for a maximum is permissible, but that even then we shall not have anything like the true relation of any particular income to the general standard of wealth in a time when England was so much smaller than our England of to-day, and in an England where wealth had been until that moment so well divided, and especially in an England where the objects both of luxury and expenditure were so utterly different to our own: where all textile fabric was, for instance, so much dearer in proportion to food than it is now, and where yet a man could earn in a few weeks' labour what would with us be capital enough to stock a small farm.

It is safe to say, however, that when Cromwell had got his young relation—whatever that relationship was—into possession of the two foundations in Huntingdon, he had set him up as a considerable local gentleman, and whether it was the inheritance of the Cromwell blood through his mother, or something equally unpleasant in the heredity of his father, Morgan, young Williams ("alias Cromwell") did not stick there.

Early in 1540 he swallowed bodily the enormous revenues of Ramsey Abbey.

Now to appreciate what that meant we must return to the case we have already established in the case of Westminster. Westminster almost alone of the great foundations remains with a certain splendour attached to it; we cannot, indeed, see all the dependencies as they used to stand to the south of the great Abbey. We cannot see the lively and populous community dependent upon it; still less can we appreciate what a figure it must have cut in the days when London was but a large country town, and when this walled monastic community stood in its full grandeur surrounded by its gardens and farms. But still, the object lesson afforded by the Abbey yet remains visible to us. We can see it as it was, and we know that its income must have represented in the England at that time infinitely more in outward effect than do to-day the largest private incomes of our English gentry: a Solomon Joel, for instance, or a Rothschild, does not occupy so great a place in modern England as did Westminster, at the close of the Middle Ages, in the very different England of its time.

Well, Ramsey was the equivalent of half Westminster, and young Williams swallowed it whole. He was not given it outright, but the price at which he bought it is significant of the way in which the monastic lands were distributed, and in which incidentally the squirearchy of England was founded. He bought it for less than three years' purchase. Where he got the money, or indeed whether he paid ready money at all, we do not know. If he did furnish the sum down we may suspect that he borrowed it from his uncle, and we may hope that that genial financier charged but a low rate of interest to one whom he had so signally favoured.

Contemporaneously with this vast accession of fortune, which made Williams the principal man in the county, Cromwell, now Earl of Essex, fell from favour, and was executed. The barony was revived for his son five months after his death and was not extinguished until the first years of the eighteenth century, but with this, the direct lineage of the King's Vicar-General, we are not concerned: our business is with the family of Williams.

Young Williams did not imitate his protector in showing any startling fidelity to the fallen. He became a courtier, was permanently in favour with the King and with the King's son, and died established in the great territorial position which he had come into by so singular an accident.

His son, Henry, maintained that position, and possibly increased it. He was four times High Sheriff of the two counties; he received Elizabeth, his sovereign and patroness, at his seat at Hinchinbrooke (one of the convents), and in general he played the rôle with which we are so tediously familiar in the case of the new and monstrous fortunes of our own times.

He was in Parliament also for the Queen, and it was his brother who moved the resolution of thanks to Elizabeth for the beheading of Mary Queen of Scots.

He died in 1603, and even to his death the alias was maintained. "Williams (alias Cromwell)" was the legal signature which guaranteed the validity of purchases and sales, while to the outer world CROMWELL (alias Williams) was the formula by which the family gently thrust itself into the tradition of another and more genteel name. The whole thing was done, like everything else this family ever did, by a mixture of trickery and patience; he obtained no special leave from Chancery as the law required; he simply used the "Williams" in public less and less and the "Cromwell" more and more. When he died, his sons after him, Robert and Oliver, had forgotten the Williams altogether—in public—and in the case of such powerful men it was convenient for the neighbours to forget the lineage also; so with the end of the sixteenth century these Williams have become Cromwells, pur et simple, and Cromwells they remain. But still the old caution clings to them where the law, and especially where money, is concerned; even Robert's son, who grew to be the Lord Protector, signs Williams when it is a case of securing his wife's dowry. Of Robert and Oliver, sons of Henry, and grandsons of the original Richard, Oliver, the elder, inherited, of course, the main wealth of the family, but Robert also was portioned, and as was invariably the case with the Williams' (alias Cromwell), the portion took the form of monastic lands.

Many more estates of the Church had come into the hands of this highly accretive family in the half century that had passed since the destruction of the monasteries. [Thus at the very end of the century we find Oliver telling the abbey land of Stratton to a haberdasher in London for £3000.]

The portion of this younger brother, Robert, consisted of religious estates in the town of Huntingdon itself, and it is highly characteristic of the whole tribe that the very house in which the Lord Protector was born was monastic, and had been, before the Dissolution, a hospital dedicated to the use of the poor. For the Lord Protector was the son of this Robert, who by a sort of atavism had added to the ample income derived from monastic spoil the profits of a brewery. It was Mrs Cromwell who looked after the brewery, and some appreciable part of the family revenues were derived from it when, in 1617, her husband died, leaving young Oliver, the future Lord Protector, an only son of eighteen, upon her hands.

The quarrels between young Oliver and old Oliver (the absurdly wealthy head of the family) would furnish material for several diverting pages, but they do not concern this, which is itself but a digression from the general subject of my book.

The object of that digression has been to trace the growth of but one great territorial family, from the gutter to affluence in the course of less than 100 years; to show how plain "Williams" gradually and secretly became "Cromwell"—because the new name had about it a flavour of nobility, however parvenu; to show how the whole of their vast revenues depended upon, and was born from, the destruction of monastic system, and to show by the example of one Thames-side family how rapidly and from what sources was derived that economic power of the squires which, when it came to the issue of arms, utterly destroyed what was left of the national monarchy.

The new régime had, however, other features about it which must not be forgotten. For instance, in this growth of a new territorial body upon the ruins of the monastic orders, in this sudden and portentous increase of the wealth and power of the squires of England, the mutability of the new system is perhaps as striking as any other of its characteristics.

Manors or portions of manors which had been steadily fixed in the possession and customs of these undying corporations for centuries pass rapidly from hand to hand, and though there is sometimes a lull in the process the uprooting reoccurs after each lull, as though continuity and a strong tradition, which are necessarily attached for good or for evil to a free peasantry, were as necessarily disregarded by a landed plutocracy. There is not, perhaps, in all Europe a similar complete carelessness for the traditions of the soil and for the attachment of a family to an ancestral piece of land as is to be found among these few thousand squires. The system remains, but the individual families, the particular lineages, appear without astonishment and are destroyed almost without regret. Aliens, Orientals and worse, enter the ruling class, and are received without surprise; names that recall the Elizabethans go out, and are not mourned.

We are accustomed to-day, when we see some village estate in our own country pass from an impoverished gentleman to some South African Jew, to speak of the passing of an old world and of its replacement by a new and a worse one. But an examination of the records which follow the Dissolution of the monasteries may temper our sorrow. The wound that was dealt in the sixteenth century to our general national traditions affected the love of the land as profoundly as it did religion, and the apparent antiquity which the trees, the stones, and a certain spurious social feeling lend to these country houses is wholly external.

Among the riparian manors of the Thames the fate of Bisham is very characteristic of the general fate of monastic land. It was surrendered, among other smaller monasteries, in 1536, though it enjoyed an income corresponding to about £6000 a year of our money, and of course very much more than £6000 a year in our modern way of looking at incomes. It was thus a wealthy place, and how it came to be included in the smaller monasteries is not quite clear. At any rate it was restored immediately after. The monks of Chertsey were housed in it, as we have already seen, and the revenues of several of the smaller dissolved houses were added to it; so that it was at the moment of its refoundation about three times as wealthy as it had been before. The prior who had surrendered in 1536, one Barlow, was made Bishop of St Asaphs, and in turn of St. Davids, Bath and Wells, and Chichester; he is that famous Barlow who took the opportunity of the Reformation to marry, and whose five daughters all in turn married the Protestant bishops of the new Church of England. But this is by the way. The fate of the land is what is interesting. From Anne of Cleves, whose portion it had been, and to whom the Government of the great nobles under Edward VI. confirmed it after Henry VIII.'s death, it passed, upon her surrendering it in 1552, to a certain Sir Philip Hoby. He had been of the Privy Council of Henry VIII. Upon his death it passed to his nephew, Edward Hoby; Edward was a Parliamentarian under Elizabeth, wrote on Divinity, and left an illegitimate son, Peregrine, to whom he bequeathed Bisham upon his death in 1617. It need hardly be said that before 100 years were over the son was already legitimatised in the county traditions; his son, Edward, was created Baron just after the Restoration, in 1666. The succession was kept up for just 100 years more, when the last male heir of the family died in 1766. He was not only a baron but a parson as well, and on his death the estate went to relatives by the name of Mill, or, as we might imagine, "Hoby" Mill. It did not long remain with them. They died out in 1780 and the Van Sittarts bought it of the widow.

Consider Chertsey, from which Bisham sprang. The utter dispersion of the whole tradition of Chertsey is more violent than that perhaps of any other historical site in England. The Crown maintained, as we have seen to be the case elsewhere, its nominal hold upon the foundations of the abbey and of what was left of the buildings, though that hold was only nominal, and it maintained such a position until 1610—that is, for a full lifetime after the community was dispersed. But the tradition created by FitzWilliam continued, and the Crown was ready to sell at that date, to a certain Dr. Hammond. The perpetual mobility which seems inseparable from spoils of this kind attaches thenceforward to the unfortunate place. The Hammonds sell after the Restoration to Sir Nicholas Carew, and before the end of the seventeenth century the Carews pass it on to the Orbys, and the Orbys pass it on to the Waytes. The Waytes sell it to a brewer of London, one Hinde. So far, contemptuous as has been the treatment of this great national centre, it had at least remained intact. With Hinde's son even that dignity deserted it. He found it advisable to distribute the land in parcels as a speculation; the actual emplacement of the building went to a certain Harwell, an East Indian, in 1753, and his son left it by will to a private soldier called Fuller, who was suspected of being his illegitimate brother. Fuller, as might be expected, saw nothing but an opportunity of making money. He redivided what was left intact of the old estate, and sold that again by lots in 1809; a stockbroker bought the remaining materials of a house whose roots struck back to the very footings of our country, sold them for what they were worth—and there was the end of Chertsey.

Then there is also Radley: which begins as an exception, but fails. It was a manor of Abingdon, and after the Dissolution it fell a prey to that one of the Seymours who proved too dirty and too much even for his brother and was put to death in 1549. It passed for the moment, as we have seen several of these riverside manors do, into the hands of Mary. But upon her death Elizabeth bestowed it upon a certain Stonehouse, and the Stonehouses did come uncommonly near to founding a family that should endure. Nor can their tradition be said to have disappeared when the name changed and the manor passed to the nephew of the last Stonehouse, by name Bowyer. But Bowyer did not retain it. He gradually ruined himself: and it is amusing at this distance of time to learn that the cause of his ruin was the idea that coal underlay his property. Everyone knows what Radley since became: it was purchased by an enthusiast, and is now a school springing from his foundation.

Or consider the two Hinkseys opposite Oxford, both portions of Abingdon manors; they are granted in the general loot to two worthies bearing the names of Owen and Bridges: a doctor.

These were probably no more than vulgar speculators upon a premium—"Stags," as we should say to-day—for a few years afterwards we find a Williams in possession of one of the Hinkseys; he is followed by the Perrots, and only quite late, and by purchase, do we come to the somewhat more dignified name of Harcourt. The other Hinksey, after still more varied adventures, ends up in the hands of the Berties, obscure south-country people who date from a rich Protestant marriage of the time.

Cholsey, again, with its immemorial traditions of unchanging ecclesiastical custom, receiving its priests in Saxon times from the

Mont St. Michel upon the marches of Brittany, and later holding as a manor from the Abbot of Reading, remains with the Crown but a very few years. In 1555 Mary handed it over to that Sir Robert Englefield who was promptly attainted by her successor. It gets in the hands of the Knowleses, then of the Rich's, and ends up with the family of Edwardes-seventeenth-century Welshmen, who, by a plan of wealthy marriages, became gentlemen, and have now for 100 years and more been peers, under the title of Kensington.

The mention of Sir Robert Englefield leads one to what is perhaps the best example in the whole Thames Valley of this perpetual chop and change in the holding of English land; that example is to be discovered at Pangbourne.

Pangbourne also was monastic; and the manor held, as did Cholsey, of Reading Abbey. In the race for the spoils Dudley clutched it in 1550. When he was beheaded, three years later, and it passed again to the Crown, Mary handed it (as she had handed Cholsey) to Sir Robert Englefield. His attainder followed. Within ten years it changes hands again. Elizabeth in 1563 gave it to her cofferer, a Mr Weldon. This personage struck no root, nor his son after him, for in 1613, while still some were alive who could remember the old custom and immemorial monastic lordship of the place, Weldon the younger sold it to a certain Davis.

Davis, one would hope—in that seventeenth century which was so essentially the century of the squires, and in that generation also wherein the squires wiped out what was left of the Crown and left the King a salaried dependant of the governing class—Davis might surely have attempted to found a family and to achieve some sort of dignity of tradition. He probably made no such an attempt, but if he did he failed; for only half-a-century later the unfortunate place changes hands again, and the Davises sell it to the Breedons.

The Breedons showed greater stability. They are actually associated with Pangbourne for over a century, but even this experiment in lineage broke down, through the extinction of the direct line. In 1776, by a sham continuity consonant to the whole recent story of English land, it passes to yet another family on the condition of their assuming the name of Breedon—which was not their own.

All up and down England, and especially in this Thames Valley, which is in all its phases so typical and symbolical of the rest of the country, this stir and change of tenure is to be found, originating with the sharp changes of 1540, and continuing to our own day.

Anywhere along this Berkshire shore of the Thames the process may be traced; even the poor little ruined nunnery of

138

Ankerwike shows it. The site of that quiet and forgotten community was seized under Edward VI. by Smith the courtier. Then you find it in the pockets of the Salters, after them of the Lysons. The Lysons sell it to the Lees, and finally it passes by marriage to the Harcourts.

The number of such examples that could be taken in the Valley of the Thames alone would be far too cumbersome for these pages. One can close the list with Sonning.

Sonning, which had been very possibly the see of an early bishopric, and which was certainly a country house of the Bishop of Salisbury, did not pass from ecclesiastical hands by a theft, but it was none the less doomed to the same mutability as the rest. In 1574 it was exchanged with the Crown for lands in Dorset. The Crown kept it for an unusually long time, considering the way in which land slipped on every side from the control of the National Government at this period. It is still royal under Charles I., but it passes in 1628 to Halstead and Chamberlain. In little more than twenty years it is in the hands of the family of Rich. Then there is a lull, just as there was in the case of Pangbourne, and a continuity that lasts throughout the eighteenth century. But just as a tradition began to form it was broken, and in the first years of the nineteenth century Sonning is sold to the Palmers.

Parallel to the rise of the squires and their capture of English government has gone the development of the English town system. And this, the last historical phase with which we shall deal in these pages, is also very well and typically illustrated in the history of the Thames Valley. That valley contains London, which is, of course, not only far the largest but in its way the fullest example of what is peculiarly English in the development of town life; and it contains, in the modern rise of Oxford and Reading, two of the very best instances to show how the English town in its modern aspect has sprung from the industrial system and from the introduction of railways. For neither has any natural facilities for production, and the growth of each in the nineteenth century has been wholly artificial.

The most recent change of all, with which these notes will end, is, one need hardly say, this industrial transformation. It has made a completely new England, and it nourishes the only civilised population in the world which is out of touch with arms, and with the physical life and nature of the country it inhabits, and the only population in which the vast majority are concerned with things of which they have no actual experience, and feel most strongly upon matters dictated to them at second or third hand by the proprietors of great journals.

What that new England will become none of us can tell; we

cannot even tell whether the considerable problem of maintaining it as an organised civilisation will or will not be solved. All the conditions are so completely new, our whole machinery of government so thoroughly presupposes a little aristocratic agricultural state, and our strong attachment to form and ritual so hampers all attempts at reorganisation, that the way in which we shall answer, if we do answer, the question of this sphinx, cannot as yet even be guessed at.

But long before the various historical causes at work had begun to produce the great modern English town, long before the use of coal, the development of the navy, and, above all, the active political transformation of our rivals during the eighteenth century, had given us that industrial supremacy which we have but recently lost, the English town was a thing with characteristics of its own in Europe.

In the first place, it was not municipal in the Roman sense. The sharp distinction which the Roman Empire and the modern French Republic, and, from the example of that republic, the whole of Western Europe, establish between town and country, comes from the fact that European thought, method of government, and the rest, were formed on the Mediterranean: but the civilisation of the Mediterranean was one of city states; the modern civilisation which has returned to Roman traditions is, therefore, necessarily municipal. A man's first country in antiquity was his town; he died for his town; he left his wealth to his town; the word "civilisation," like the word "citizen," and like a hundred words connected with the superiority of mankind, are drawn from the word for a town. To be political, to possess a police, to recognise boundaries—all this was to be a townsman, and the various districts of the Empire took their proper names, at least, from the names of their chief cities, as do to-day the French and the Italian countrysides.

Doubtless in Roman times the governing forces of Britain attempted a similar system here. But it does not seem ever to have taken root in the same way that it did beyond the Channel. The absence of a municipal system in the fullest sense is one of the very few things which differentiates the Roman Britain from the rest of the Empire, others being a land frontier to the west, and the large survival of aboriginal dialects.

The Roman towns were not small, indeed Roman London was very large; they were not ill connected with highroads; they were certainly wealthy and full of commerce; but they gave their names to no districts, and their municipal institutions have left but very faint traces upon posterity.

The barbarian invasions fell severely upon the Roman cities of

140

Britain, in some very rare cases they may have been actually destroyed, but in the much more numerous cases where we may be reasonably sure that municipal life continued without a break throughout the incursions of the pirates, their decay was pitiful; and when recorded history begins again, after a gap of two hundred years, with the Roman missionaries of the sixth and seventh centuries, we find thenceforward, and throughout the Saxon period, many of the towns living the life of villages.

The proportion that were walled was much smaller than was the case upon the Continent, and even the most enduring emblem and the most tenacious survival of the Roman Imperial system— namely, the Bishop seated in the chief municipality of his district— was not universal to English life.

It is characteristic of Gregory the Great that he intended, or is believed to have intended, Britain, when he had recivilised it, to be set out upon a clear Latin model, with a Primate in the chief city and suffragans in every other. But if he had such a plan (and it would have been a typically Latin plan) he must have been thinking of a Britain very different from that which his envoys actually found. When the work was accomplished the little market town of Canterbury was the seat of the Primate; the old traditions of York secured for it a second archbishop, great London could not be passed over, but small villages in some places, insignificant boroughs in others, were the sites of cathedrals. Selsey, a rural manor or fishing hamlet, was the episcopal centre of St. Wilfrid and his successors in their government of Sussex; Dorchester, as we have seen, was the episcopal town, or rather village, for something like half England. In the names of its officers also and in the methods of their government the Anglo-Saxon town was agricultural.

With the advent of the Normans, as one might expect, municipal life to some extent re-arose. But it still maintained its distinctively English character throughout the Middle Ages. Contrast London or Oxford, for instance, in the twelfth and early thirteenth centuries, with contemporary Paris. In London and Oxford the wall is built once for all, and when it is completed the town may grow into suburbs as much as it likes, no new wall is built. In Paris, throughout its history, as the town grows, the first concern of its Government is to mark out new limits which shall sharply define it from the surrounding country. Philip Augustus does it, a century and a half later Etienne Marcel did it; through the seventeenth century, and the eighteenth, the custom is continued: through the nineteenth also, and to-day new and strict limits are about to be imposed on the expanded city.

Again the metropolitan idea, which is consonant to, and the climax of, a municipal system, is absent from the story of English towns.

Until a good hundred years after the Conquest you cannot say where the true capital of England is, and when you find it at last in London, the King's Court is in a suburb outside the walls and the Parliament of a century later yet meets at Westminster and not in the City.

The English judges are not found fixed in local municipal centres, they are itinerant. The later organisation of the Peace does not depend upon the county towns; it is an organisation of rural squires; and, most significant of all, no definite distinction can ever be drawn between the English village and the English town neither in spirit nor in legal definition. You have a town like Maidenhead, which has a full local Government, and yet which has no mayor for centuries. Conversely, a town having once had a mayor may dwindle down into a village, and no one who respects English tradition bothers to interfere with the anomaly. For instance, you may to-day in Orford enjoy the hospitality, or incur the hostility, of a Mayor and Corporation.

On all these accounts the banks of the Thames, until quite the latest part of our historical development, presented a line of settlements in which it was often difficult to draw the distinction between the village and the town.

Consider also this characteristic of the English thing, that the boroughs sending Members to Parliament first sent them quite haphazard and then by prescription.

Simon de Montfort gets just a few borough Members to his Parliament because he knows they will be on his side; and right down to the Tudors places are enfranchised—as, for example, certain Cornish boroughs were—not because they are true towns but because they will support the Government. Once returning Members, the place has a right to return them, until the partial reform of 1832. It is a right like the hereditary right of a peer, a quaint custom. It has no relation to municipal feeling, for municipal feeling does not exist. Old Sarum may lose every house, Gatton may retain but seven freeholders, yet each solemnly returns its two Members to Parliament.

From the first records that we possess until the beginning of the nineteenth century, the line of the Thames was a string of large villages and small towns, differing in size and wealth far less than their descendants do to-day. In this arrangement, of course, the valley was similar to all the rest of England, but perhaps the prosperity of the larger villages and the frequency of the market towns was more marked on the line of the Thames than in any other countryside, from the permanent influx of wealth due to the royal castles, the great monastic foundations, and the continual stream of travel to and from London which bound the whole together.

Cricklade, Lechlade, Oxford, Abingdon, Dorchester, Wallingford, Reading, and Windsor—old Windsor, that is—were considerable places from at least the period of the Danish invasions. They formed the objective of armies, or the subject matter of treaties or important changes. But the first standard of measure which we can apply is that given us by the Norman Survey.

How indecisive is that standard has already been said. We do not accurately know what categories of wealth were registered in Domesday. The Anglo-Saxon Chronicle, barbaric in this as in most other matters, would have it that the Survey was complete, and applied to all the landed fortune of England. That, of course, is absurd. But we do have a rough standard of comparison for rural manors, though it is a very rough one. Though we cannot tell how much of the measurements and of the numbers given are conventional and how much are real, though we do not know whether the plough-lands referred to are real fields or merely measures of capacity for production, though historians are condemned to ceaseless guessing upon every term of the document, and though the last orthodox guess is exploded every five or six years—yet when we are told that one manor possessed so many ploughs or paid upon so many hides, or had so many villein holdings while another manor had but half or less in each category; and when we see the dues, say three times as large in the first as in the second, then we can say with certitude that the first was much more important than the second; how much more important we cannot say. We can, to repeat an argument already advanced, affirm the inhabitants of any given manor to be at the very least not less than five times the number of holdings, and thus fix a minimum everywhere. For instance, we can be certain that William's rural England had not less than 2,000,000, though we cannot say how much more they may not have been—3,000,000, 4,000,000, or 5,000,000. In agricultural life—that is, in the one industry of the time—Domesday does afford a vague statement to the rural conditions of England at the end of the eleventh century, and, dark as it is, no other European nation possesses such a minute record of its economic origins.

But with the towns the case is different. There, except for the minimum of population, we are quite at sea. We may presume that the houses numbered are only the houses paying tax, or at least we may presume this in some cases, but already the local customs of each town were so highly differentiated that it is quite impossible to

143

say with certitude what the figures may mean. It is usual to take the taxable value of the place to the Crown and to establish a comparison on that basis, but it is perhaps wiser, though almost as inconclusive, to consider each case, and all the elements of it separately, and to attempt, by a co-ordination of the different factors given to arrive at some sort of scale.

Judged in this manner, Wallingford and Oxford are the early towns of the Thames Valley which afford the best subjects for survey.

Wallingford in Domesday counted, closes and cottages together, just under 500 units of habitation. It is, of course, a matter of conjecture how much population this would stand for. A minimum is here, as elsewhere, easily established. We may presuppose that a close, even of the largest kind, was but a private one; we may next average the inhabitants of each house at five, which is about the average of modern times, and so arrive at a population of 2500. But this minimum of 2500 for the population of Wallingford at the time of the Conquest is too artificial and too full of modern bias to be received. Not even the strongest prejudice in favour of underrating the wealth and population of early England, a prejudice which has for it objects the emphasising of our modern perfection, would admit so ludicrous a conclusion. But while we may be perfectly certain that the population of Wallingford was far larger than this minimum, to obtain a maximum is not so easy. We do not know, with absolute certainty, whether the whole of the town has been enumerated in the Survey, though we have a better ground for supposing it in this case than in most others. Such numerous details are given of holdings which, though situated in the town, counted in the property of local manors that we are fairly safe in saying that we have here a more than commonly complete survey. The very cottages are mentioned, as, for example, "twenty-two cottages outside the wall," and their condition is described in terms which, though not easy for us to understand, clearly signify that they could be taken as paying the full tax.

The real elements of uncertainty lie, first in the number of people normally inhabiting one house at that time, and secondly, in the exact meaning of the word "haga" or "close."

As to the first point, we may take it that one household of five would be the least, ten would be the most, to be present under the roof of an isolated family; but we must remember that the Middle Ages contained in their social system a conception of community which not only appeared (and is still remembered) in connection with monastic institutions, but which inspired the whole of military and civil life. To put it briefly, a man at the time of the Conquest,

144

and for centuries later, would rather have lived as part of a community than as an individual householder, and conversely, those indices of importance and social position which we now estimate in furniture and other forms of ostentation were then to be found in the number of dependants surrounding the head of the house. A merchant, for example, if he flourished, was the head of a very numerous community; every parish church in a town represented a society of priests and of their servants, and of course a garrison (such as Wallingford pre-eminently possessed) meant a very large community indeed. We are usually safe, at any rate in the towns, if we multiply the known number of tenements by ten in order to arrive at the number of souls inhabiting the borough. To give the Wallingford of the Conquest a minimum of 5000, if we were certain that 500 (or, to speak exactly, 491) was the number of single units of taxation within the borough, would be to set that minimum quite low enough.

The second difficulty is that of establishing the meaning of the word "haga." In some cases it may represent one single large establishment. But on the other hand we can point to six which between them covered a whole acre, and no one with the least acquaintance of mediæval municipal topography, no one, for instance, who knows the history of twelfth-century Paris, would allow one-sixth of an acre to a single average house within the walls of a town. A close would have one or more wells, it is true; some closes certainly would have gardens, but the labour of fortification, and the privilege of market, were each of them causes which forbade any great extension of open spaces, save in the case of privileged or wealthy communities or individuals.

From what we know of closes elsewhere, it is more probable that these at Wallingford were the "cells" as it were of the borough organism. A man would be granted in the first growth of the town a unit of land with definitely established boundaries, which he would probably enclose (the word "haga" refers to such an enclosure), and though at first there might be only one house upon it, it would be to his interest to multiply the tenements within this unit, which unit rendered a regular, customary and unchanging due to its various superiors, whatever the number of inhabitants it grew to contain.

If we turn to a comparison based upon taxation we have equal difficulties, though difficulties of a different sort. We saw in the case of Old Windsor that a community of perhaps 1000, probably of more, but at any rate something more like a large village than a town (and one moreover not rated as a town), paid in dues the equivalent of thirty loads of wheat. Wallingford paid the equivalent of only twenty or twenty-two. But on the other hand the total Farm of the Borough, the globular price at which the taxes could be reckoned upon to yield a profit, was equivalent to no less than 400 such loads.

Judged by the number of hagæ we should have a Wallingford about five times the size of Old Windsor. Judged by the taxable capacity we should have an Old Wallingford of more than ten times the size of Old Windsor.

Here again a further element of complexity enters. It was quite out of the spirit of the Middle Ages to estimate dues, whether to a feudal superior or to the National Government, or even minor payments made to a true proprietorial owner at the full capacity of the economic unit concerned. All such payment was customary. Even where, in the later Middle Ages, a man indubitably owned (in our modern sense of the word "owned") a piece of freehold land, and let it (in our modern sense of the word "let"), it would not have occurred to him or his tenant that the very highest price obtainable for the productive capacity of the land should be paid. The philosophy permeating the whole of society compelled the owner and the tenant, even in this extreme case, to a customary arrangement; for it was an arrangement intended to be permanent, to allow for wide fluctuations of value, and therefore to be necessarily a minimum. If this was the case in the later Middle Ages where undoubted proprietary right was concerned, still more was it the case in the early Middle Ages with the customary feudal dues; these varied infinitely from place to place, rising in scale from those of privileged communities wholly exempt to those of places such as we believe Old Windsor to have been, which paid (and these were the exceptions), not indeed every penny that they could pay (as they would now have to pay a modern landlord), but half, or perhaps more than half, such a rent.

Where Wallingford stood in this scale it is quite impossible to say, and we can only conclude with the very general statement that the Wallingford of the Conquest consisted of certainly more than 5000 souls, more probably of 10,000, and quite possibly of more than 10,000.

Having taken Wallingford with its minute and valuable record as a sort of unit, we can roughly compare it with other centres of populations upon the river at the same date.

Old Windsor we have already dealt with, and made it out from a fifth to a tenth of Wallingford. Reading was apparently far smaller. Indeed Reading is one of the puzzles of the early history of the Thames Valley. We have already seen in discussing these strategical points upon the river what advantages it had, and yet it appears only sporadically in ancient history as a military post. The Danes hold it on the first occasion on which we find the site recorded, in the latter half of the ninth century: it has a castle during the anarchy of the twelfth, but it is a castle which soon disappears. It frequently plays a part in the Civil Wars of the seventeenth, but the part it plays is only temporary.

And Reading presents a similar puzzle on the civilian side. It is situated at the junction of two waterways, one of which leads directly from the Thames Valley to the West of England, yet it does not seem to have been of a considerable civil importance until the establishment of its monastery; and even then it is not a town of first-class size or wealth, nor does it take up its present position until quite late in the history of the country.

At the time of the Domesday Survey it actually counts, in the number of recorded enclosures at least, for less than a third of Old Windsor; and we may take it, after making every allowance for possible omissions or for some local custom which withdrew it from the taxing power of the Crown, for little more than a village at that moment.

The size of Oxford at the same period we have already touched upon, but since, like every other inference founded upon Domesday, the matter has become a subject of pretty violent discussion, it will bear, perhaps, a repeated and more detailed examination at this place.

Let us first remember that the latest prejudice from which our historical school has suffered, and one which still clings to its more orthodox section, was to belittle as far as possible the general influence of European civilisation upon England; to exalt, for example, the Celtic missionaries and their work at the expense of St Augustine, to grope for shadowy political origins among the pirates of the North Sea, to trace every possible etymology to a barbaric root, and to make of Roman England and of early Medieval England—that is, of the two Englands which were most fully in touch with the general life of Europe—as small a thing as might be.

In the light of this prejudice, which is the more bitter because it is closely connected with religion and with the bitter theological passions of our universities, we are always safe in taking the larger as against the smaller modern estimates of wealth, of population and of influence, where either of these civilisations is concerned, and, conversely, we are always safe in taking at the lowest modern estimate the numbers and effect of the barbaric element in our history.

To return to the ground we have already briefly covered, and to establish a comparison with Wallingford, the word "haga," which we saw to be of such doubtful value in the case of Wallingford, is

147

replaced in Oxford by the word "mansio." The taxable units so enumerated are just over 600, but of these much more than half are set down as untaxable or imperfectly taxable under the epithets "Uasta," "Uastæ." What that epithet means we do not know. It may mean anything between "out of repair," "excused from taxation because they do not come up to our new standard of the way in which a house in a borough should be kept up, and because we want to give them time to put themselves in order," down to the popular acceptation of the word as meaning "ruined," or even "destroyed."

We know that at the close of the eleventh century, or indeed at any time before the thirteenth, the small man who lived under his own roof would live in a very low house, and that, space for space of ground area, the cubical contents of these poor dwellings would be less than those of modern slums. On the other hand, we know that the population would live much more in the open air, slept much more huddled, and also that a very considerable proportion—what proportion we cannot say, but probably quite half of a Norman borough—was connected with the huge communal institutions—military, ecclesiastical, and for that matter mercantile, as well—which marked the period. We know that the occupied space stood for very much what is now enclosed by the line of the old walls, and we know that under modern conditions this space, in spite of our great empty public buildings, our sparsely inhabited wealthy houses, and our college gardens, can comfortably hold some 5000 people. We can say, therefore, at a guess, but only at a guess, that the Oxford of the Conquest must have had some 3000 people in it at the very least, and can hardly have had 10,000 at the most. These are wide limits, but anyone who shall pretend to make them narrower is imposing upon his readers with an appearance of positive knowledge which is the charlatanism of the colleges, and pretends to exact knowledge where he possesses nothing but the vague basis of antiquarian conjecture.

It is sufficiently clear (and the reading of any of our most positive modern authorities upon Domesday will make it clearer) that no sort of statistical exactitude can be arrived at for the population of the boroughs in the early Middle Ages. But when we consider that Reading is certainly underestimated, and when we consider the detail in which we are informed of Old Windsor, Wallingford, and Oxford, with the neglect of Abingdon, Lechlade, Cricklade, and Dorchester, one can roughly say that the Thames above London possessed in Staines, Windsor, Cookham, probably Henley, perhaps Bensington, Dorchester, Eynsham, and possibly Buscot, large villages varying from some hundreds in population to a little over 1000, not defended, not reckoned as towns, and

148

agricultural in character. To these we may add Chertsey, Ealing, and a few others whose proximity to London makes it difficult for us to judge except in the vaguest way their true importance.

In another category, possessing a different type of communal life, already thinking of themselves as towns, we should have Cricklade, Lechlade, Abingdon, and Kingston among the smaller, though probably possessing a population not much larger than that of the larger villages; while of considerable centres there were but three: Reading the smallest, almost a town, but one upon which we have no true or sufficient data; Wallingford the largest, with the population of a flourishing county town in our own days, and Oxford, a place which, though in worse repair, ran Wallingford close.

Henley affords an interesting study. At the time of the Conquest, Bensington was no longer, Henley not yet, a borough. To trace the growth of Henley is especially engrossing, because it is one of the very rare examples of a process which earlier generations of historians, and notably the popular historians like Freeman and the Rev. Mr Green, took to be a common feature in the story of this island. They were wrong, of course, and they have been widely and deservedly ridiculed for imagining that the greater part of our English boroughs grew up since the barbarian invasions upon waste places. On the contrary most of our towns grew up upon Roman and pre-Roman foundations, and are continuous with the pre-historic past. But Henley forms a very interesting exception.

It was a hamlet which went with the manor of Bensington, and that point alone is instructive, for it points to the insignificance of the place. When the lords of Bensington went hunting up on Chiltern they found on the far side of the hill, it may be presumed, a little clearing near the river. This was all that Henley was, and it is probable that even the church of the place was not built until quite late in the Christian period; there is at any rate an old tradition that Aldeburgh is the mother of Henley, and it is imagined by those who wrote monographs upon the locality that this tradition points to the church of Aldeburgh as the mother church of what was at first a chapel upon the riverside.

When we first hear of Henley it is already called a town, and the date of this is the first year of King John, 1199.

It must be remembered that the river had been developed and changed in that first century of orderly government under the Normans. Indeed one of the reforms which the aristocracy made much of in their revolt, and which is granted in Magna Charta, is the destruction of the King's weirs upon the Thames. But the weirs cannot have been permanently destroyed; though the public rights

149

over the river were curtailed by Magna Charta, the system of regulation was founded and endured. It is probably this improvement on the great highway which led to the growth of Henley, and when Reading Minster had become the great thing it was late in the twelfth century, Henley must have felt the effect, for it would have afforded the nearest convenient stage down the river from the new and wealthy settlement round the Cluniac Abbey. In the thirteenth century—that is, in the first hundred years after the earliest mention we have of the place—Henley became rapidly more and more important. It seems to have afforded a convenient halting place whenever progress was made up river, especially a royal progress from Windsor. Edward I. stayed there constantly, and we possess a record of three dates which are very significant of this kind of journey. In the December of 1277 the King goes up river. On the sixteenth of the month he slept at Windsor, on the seventeenth at Henley, the next day at Abingdon; and in his son's time Henley has grown so much that it counts as one of the three only boroughs in the whole of Oxfordshire: Oxford and Woodstock are the two others.

It was in the thirteenth century also that a bridge was thrown across the river at this point—that is, Henley possessed a bridge long before Wallingford, and at a time when the river could be crossed by road in but very few places. The granting of a number of indulgences, and the promises of masses in the middle of the thirteenth century for this object, give us the date; and, what is perhaps equally interesting, this early bridge was of stone.

It is usual to think of the early bridges over the Thames as wooden bridges. Aft older generation was accustomed to many that still remained. This was true of the later Middle Ages, and of the torpor and neglect in building which followed the Reformation. But it was not true of the thirteenth and fourteenth centuries. The bridge at Henley, like the bridge of Wallingford and the later bridge of Abingdon, was of stone.

It was allowed to fall into decay, and when Leland crossed the river at this point it was upon a wooden bridge, the piers of which stood upon the old foundation. How long that wooden bridge had existed in 1533, when Leland noticed it, we cannot tell, but it remained of wood until 1786, when the present bridge replaced it.

In spite of the early importance of the town, it was not regularly incorporated for a long time, but was governed by a Warden, the first on the list being the date of 1305, within the reign of Edward I. The charter which gave Henley a Mayor and Corporation was granted as late as the reign of Henry VIII. and but a few years before Leland's visit. From that moment, however, the town ceased to expand, either in importance or in numbers; the destruction of Reading Abbey and of the Cell of Westminster at Hurley just over the river, very possibly affected its prosperity. At the beginning of the nineteenth century it had a population of less than 3000, and sixty years later it had not added another 1000 to that number.

Maidenhead follows, for centuries, a sort of parallel course to the development of Henley.

Recently, of course, it has very largely increased in population, and in this it is an example in a minor degree of what Reading and Oxford are in a major degree—that is, of the changes which the railway has made in the Thames Valley. But until the effect of the railway began to be felt Maidenhead was the younger and parallel town to Henley.

For example, though we cannot tell exactly when Maidenhead Bridge was built, we may suppose it to have been some few years after Henley Bridge. It already exists and is in need of repair in 1297. Henley Bridge is founded more than a generation earlier than that.

"Maidenhythe," as it was called, has been thought to have been before the building of this bridge a long timber wharf upon the river, but that is only a guess. There must have been some local accumulation of wealth or of traffic or it would not have been chosen as a site for the new bridge which was somewhat to divert the western road.

Originally, so far as we can judge, the main stream of gravel crossed the Thames at Cookham, and again at Henley. Why this double crossing should have been necessary it is useless to conjecture unless one hazards the guess that the quality of the soil in very early times gave so much better going upon the high southern bank of the river that it was worth while carrying the main road along the bank, even at the expense of a double crossing of the stream. If that was the case it is difficult to see how a town of the importance of Marlow could have grown up upon the farther shore; that Marlow was important we know from the fact that it had a Borough representation in Parliament in the first years of that experiment before the close of the thirteenth century.

At any rate, whatever the reason was, whether from some prehistoric conditions having brought the road across the peninsula at this point, or, as is more likely, on account of some curious arrangement of mediæval privilege, it is fairly certain that, in the centuries before the great development of the thirteenth, travel did come across the river in front of Cookham, recross it in front of Henley, and so make over the Chilterns to the great main bridge at

Wallingford, which led out to the Vale of the White Horse and the west country.

The importance of Cookham in this section of the road is shown in several ways. First the great market, in Domesday bringing in customary dues to the King of twenty shillings—and what twenty shillings means in Domesday in mere market dues one can appreciate by considering that all the dues from Old Windsor only amounted to ten pounds. Then again it was a royal manor which, unlike most of the others, was never alienated; it was not even alienated during the ruin and breakdown of the monarchy which followed the Dissolution of the monastic orders.

To this day traces remain of the road which joined this market to the second crossing at Henley.

We may presume that the importance of Cookham was maintained for some two centuries after the Conquest, until it was outflanked and the stream of its traffic diverted by the building of the bridge at Maidenhead.

Just as this bridge came later than the Bridge at Henley, so it was inferior to it in structure; it was, as we have seen, of timber, but such as it was, it was the cause of the growth of Maidenhead much more than was the bridge at Henley the cause of the growth of Henley. The first nucleus of municipal government grows up in connection with the Bridge Guild; the Warden and the Bridge Masters remain the head of the embryonic corporation throughout the sixteenth and seventeenth centuries, and even when the town is incorporated (shortly before the close of the seventeenth century), by James II., the maintenance and guardianship of the wooden bridge remained one of the chief occupations of the new corporation.

It was just after the granting of the Charter that the army of William III. marched across this bridge on its way to London, an episode which shows how completely Maidenhead held the monopoly of the Western road. The present stone bridge was not built to replace the old wooden one until the last quarter of the eighteenth century, parallel in this as in everything else to the example of Henley; and this position of inferiority to Henley, and of parallel advance to that town, is further seen in the statistics of population. In 1801, when Henley already boasted nearly 2000 souls, Maidenhead counted almost exactly half that number. The later growth of the place is quite modern.

The antiquity of the crossing of the Thames at Cookham is supported by a certain amount of pre-historic evidence, worth about as much as such evidence ever is, and about as little. Two Neolithic flint knives have been found there, a bronze dagger sheath and

152

spear-head, a bronze sword, and a whole collection or store of other bronze spear-heads. Such as it is, it is a considerable collection for one spot.

Cookham has not only these pre-historic remains; it has also fragments of British pottery found in the relics of pile dwellings near the river, and two Roman vases from the bed of the stream; it has further furnished Anglo-Saxon remains, and, indeed, there are very few points upon the river where so regular a continuity of the historic and the pre-historic is to be discovered as in the neighbourhood of this old ford.

In was in the course of the Middle Ages, and after the Conquest, that new Windsor rose to importance. It is not recognised as a borough before the close of the thirteenth century; it is incorporated in the fifteenth.

Reading certainly increased considerably with the continual stream of wealth that poured from the abbey; it possessed in practice a working corporation before the Dissolution, was famous for its cloth long before, and had become, in the process of years, an important town that rivalled the great monastery which had developed it; indeed it is probable that only the privileges, the conservatism, of the abbey forbade it to be recognised and chartered before the Reformation.

Abingdon also grew (but with less vigour), also had a manufactory of cloth, though of a smaller kind, and was also worthy of incorporation at the end of the Middle Ages.

Staines cannot take its place with these, for in spite of its high strategical value, of its old Roman tradition, of its proximity to London and the rest, Staines was throughout the Middle Ages, and till long after, rather a village than a town. Though a wealthy place it is purely agricultural in the Domesday Survey, and the comparative insignificance of the spot is perhaps explained by the absence of a bridge. That absence is by no means certain. Staines after all was on the great military highway leading from London westward, and it must have been necessary for considerable forces to cross the river here throughout the Dark Ages and the early Middle Ages, as did for instance, at the very close of that period, the barons on their way to Runnymede; and far earlier the army that marched hurriedly from London to intercept the Danes in 1009, when the pagans were coming up the river, and whether by the help of the tide or what not, managed to get ahead of the intercepting force. But if a bridge existed so early as the Conquest, we have no mention of it. The first allusion to a bridge is in the granting of three oaks from Windsor for the repairing of it in 1262. It may have existed long before that date, but it is significant that in the Escheats of Edward III., and as late as the twenty-fourth year of his reign—that is, after the middle of the fourteenth century—it is mentioned that the bridge existed since the reign of Henry III., which would convey the impression that in 1262 the bridge had first needed repairing, being built, perhaps, in the earlier years of the reign and completed, possibly, but a little after the death of King John.

This bridge of Staines was most unfortunate. It broke down again and again. Even an experiment in stone at the end of the last century was a failure, because the foundations did not go deep enough into the bed of the river. An iron absurdity succeeded the stone, and luckily broke down also, until at last, in the thirties of the nineteenth century, the whole thing was rebuilt, 200 yards above the old traditional site.

Staines is of interest in another way, because it marks one of those boundaries between the maritime and the wholly inland part of a river which is in so many of the English valleys associated with some important crossing. The jurisdiction of the port of London over the river extended as high as the little island just opposite the mouth of the Colne. On this island can still be seen the square stone shaft which is at least as old as the thirteenth century (though it stands on more modern steps), and which marks this limit, as it does also the shire mark between Middlesex and Buckingham.

We have, after the Dissolution it is true, and when the financial standing of most of these places had been struck a heavy blow, a valuable estimate for many of them in the inquiry ordered by Pole in 1555. This estimate gives Abingdon less than 1500 of population, Reading less than 3000, Windsor about 1000; and in general one may say that with the sixteenth century, whether the population was diminishing (as certainly contemporary witnesses believed), or whether it had increased beyond the maximum which England had seen before the Black Death, at any rate the relative importance of the various centres of population had not very greatly changed during those long five centuries of customary rule and of firm tradition. The towns and villages which Shakespeare would have passed in a journey up the river, though probably shrunk somewhat from what they had been in, let us say, the days of Edward I. or of his grandson, when the Middle Ages were in their full vigour and before the Black Death had ruined our countrysides, were still a string of some such large villages and small walled boroughs as his ancestry had seen for many hundred years, disfigured only and changed by the scaffolded ruins here and there of the great religious foundations. Windsor, Wallingford, Reading, Abingdon, and even Oxford, were towns appearing to him much as Lechlade to-day remains or Abingdon still. As for the riverside

154

villages their agricultural and native population was certainly larger than that which they now possess; and in general the effect produced upon such a journey was of a sort of even distribution of population gradually increasing from the loneliness of the upper river to the growing sites between Windsor and London, but in no part exaggerated; larger everywhere in proportion to the importance of the stream, or of agricultural or of strategical position, and forming together one united countryside, bound together even in its architecture by the common commerce of the river.

The seventeenth and eighteenth centuries did little to disturb this equilibrium or to destroy this even tradition. The opening up of the waterways and the great improvement of the highroads, and the building of bridges, and the expansion of wealth at the end of the eighteenth century had indeed some considerable effect in increasing the population of England as a whole, but the smaller country towns, in the south at least, and in the Thames Valley, seem to have benefited fairly equally from the general change. The new canals, entering at Oxford and at Reading, gave a certain lead to both those centres, and even the Severn Canal, entering at Lechlade, did a little for that up-river town. The new fashion of the public schools (which had now long been captured by the wealthier classes) also increased the importance of Eton, and towards the close of the period the now rapidly expanding capital had overfed the villages within reach of London with a considerable accession of population. But it is remarkable how evenly spread was even this industrial development.

The twin towns of Abingdon and Reading, for instance, twin monasteries, twin corporations, had for all these centuries preserved their ratio of the up-country town and the larger centre that was the neighbour of London and Windsor. In the beginning of the nineteenth century, in spite of the general increase of population, that ratio was still well preserved: it is about three to one. But the Railway found one and left the other.

The Railway came, and in our own generation that ratio began to change out of all knowledge. It grows from four, five, six, to seven to one. After a short halt you have eight, nine and at last—after eighty years—more than ten to one. The last census (that of 1901) is still more significant: Abingdon positively declines, and the last ratio is twelve.

It is through the Railway, and even then long after its first effect might have been expected, that the Valley of the Thames, later than any other wealthy district in England, loses, as all at last are doomed to lose, its historic tradition, and suffers the social revolution which has made modern England the unique and perilous thing it is among the nations of the world.

155